BRITAIN'S BEST POLITICAL CARTOONS 2019

Dr Tim Benson is Britain's leading authority on political cartoons. He runs the Political Cartoon Gallery and Café which is located near the River Thames in Putney. He has produced numerous books on the history of cartoons, including *David Low Censored*, *Giles's War*, *Churchill in Caricature*, *Low and the Dictators*, *The Cartoon Century: Modern Britain through the Eyes of Its Cartoonists*, *Drawing the Curtain: The Cold War in Cartoons* and *Over the Top: A Cartoon History of Australia at War*.

BRITAIN'S BEST POLITICAL CARTOONS 2019

Edited by Tim Benson

HUTCHINSON
LONDON

For Annabel

1 3 5 7 9 10 8 6 4 2

Hutchinson
20 Vauxhall Bridge Road
London SW1V 2SA

Hutchinson is part of the Penguin Random House
group of companies whose addresses can be found
at global.penguinrandomhouse.com.

First published in the United Kingdom by Hutchinson in 2019

www.penguin.co.uk

A CIP catalogue record for this book is available from the British Library.

ISBN 9781786331977

Typeset in 11/15.5 pt Amasis MT Light by Jouve (UK), Milton Keynes

Printed and bound by L.E.G.O. S.p.A.

Penguin Random House is committed to a sustainable future
for our business, our readers and our planet. This book is made from
Forest Stewardship Council® certified paper.

INTRODUCTION

In April 2019, the international edition of the *New York Times* published a controversial cartoon. It showed a blind Donald Trump, wearing a skullcap, being led by a guide dog – which had the face of Israeli Prime Minister Benjamin Netanyahu. The backlash was immediate. The president's son, Donald Trump Jr, condemned the cartoon for 'flagrant antisemitism', and within hours the *NYT* had apologised and deleted the image from its website.

That was only the beginning. A month and a half later, the international *NYT* announced that it would no longer publish cartoons at all. The *NYT* said it had been considering taking the leap 'for well over a year'. But there was outrage when one former *NYT* cartoonist, Patrick Chappatte, said the decision was linked with the antisemitism storm. Most cartoonists agreed that the original cartoon was ill-judged, but said that dropping cartoons altogether was excessive. The *Guardian*'s Martin Rowson denounced the *NYT* for 'its intoxicating combination of cowardice, pomposity, over-

reaction and hypocrisy'. The *Washington Post* cartoonist, Ann Telnaes, went one further, cancelling her subscription altogether. For many cartoonists, the whole saga amounted to censorship, an attack both on their art form and on political satire in general.

The incident raised a few questions that cartoonists (and cartoon historians like myself) increasingly have to grapple with. Should cartoonists be free to draw what they like? If not, what are the limits on what they can get away with? These issues have been thrown into stark relief by a number of controversial stories over the last few years. Feelings had already been running high among cartoonists thanks to the sacking of Rob Rogers by the *Pittsburgh Post-Gazette*, after 25 years as their editorial cartoonist. The newspaper had adopted a more pro-Republican outlook after a change in ownership. Rogers said that the new management did not approve of his attacks on President Trump (for its part, the *Post-Gazette* said that Rogers had become unwilling

Cartoonists have always had to deal with demanding editors – as David Low discovered when his Hitler and Mussolini-themed cartoon strip, 'Hit and Muss', caused a diplomatic row in 1939. The pro-appeasement foreign secretary, Lord Halifax, asked Low to tone down his cartoons.

to 'cooperate', and that they had never asked him to draw pro-Trump cartoons). The sacking left Rogers feeling miffed: 'When I was hired in 1993, the *Post-Gazette* was the liberal newspaper in town,' he said. Then, in July 2019, the *Guardian*'s Steve Bell sent an email to all staff at the newspaper saying that editors had refused to publish one of his cartoons, in which Labour Deputy Leader Tom Watson described Benjamin Netanyahu as an 'antisemitic trope'. 'Does the *Guardian* no longer tolerate content that runs counter to its editorial line?' he asked.

The truth is, while many cartoonists like to think of themselves as completely independent, they are invariably constrained by the publications that employ them. As the American journalist A. J. Liebling once observed, the freedom of the press has always been limited to those who own one. Newspapers are fully within their rights to control the editorial direction, and to instruct their employees – whether journalists, sub-editors, photographers or cartoonists – to fall in line.

In practice, this means every cartoonist is kept in check by an editor. *The Times*'s Peter Brookes, probably Britain's most distinguished political cartoonist, says the editor's decision is final. 'No editor needs to put up with a cartoonist who does not take notice of what he says, otherwise what's the point of an editor?' he argues. The *Evening Standard*'s Christian Adams agrees: while in the nineteenth century 'political satirists produced their cartoons as individual prints, to be perused in coffee houses completely removed from any form of editorial interference', those days have long since passed. 'Editorial cartoonists are by their very nature employees of newspapers,' he says. 'They are not, and never have been, an independent voice completely free of editorial control.'

David Low's cartoon tribute to his favourite editor, Percy Cudlipp.

The relationship between cartoonist and editor is integral to producing good work. There must be a constant dialogue, and a mutually trusting relationship. The *Observer*'s Chris Riddell believes that the key is to work face-to-face with your editor in the newspaper office: 'Once he says "yes" to a cartoon, it goes into the paper.' A historical example makes the point clear: it was no coincidence that the greatest cartoonist of the twentieth century, David Low, produced the best cartoons of his career under his favourite editor, the *Evening Standard*'s Percy Cudlipp. Low once explained why Cudlipp was a cartoonist's dream. He 'was that rare phenomenon, an editor who knew what a political cartoon was and how to present it'. This made everything easier: 'We were, so to speak, on the same wave-length. With him ideas flowed. When we met for a mug of tea once a week, sparks flew.' The story shows that even the greatest ever cartoonists were happy to take an edit or two.

What are the red lines that cartoonists are not allowed to cross? The first major constraint is a political one. The editor's job is to keep cartoons roughly in line with the outlook of their employer. In the words of the *Independent*'s Dave Brown, all cartoons should 'afflict the comfortable and comfort the afflicted'. But precisely what this means depends on a newspaper's political outlook. For example, a *Telegraph* reader might enjoy Patrick Blower's acerbic treatment of Jeremy Corbyn; a *Guardian* reader would likely not. Similarly, a newspaper that aims to straddle the political divide – such as the *Evening Standard*, read by commuters in London of all political persuasions – is more likely to offer a 'plague on all your houses' approach: Christian Adams aims to equally offend people of all political sympathies. This is just part of the fine line that all newspapers walk. If they're getting it right, readers will see their political views reflected in their newspaper of preference.

Is this censorship? Hardly. It's just newspapers doing what newspapers do: adopting a political stance, and feeding it back to their readers. To my mind, some of the recent storms around the so-called 'censoring' of cartoonists are annoying because this criticism is so one-sided. For example, when cartoonists who oppose Donald Trump – like Rob Rogers – lose their jobs, it is claimed to be a threat to free speech. But when those who are supportive of Trump are fired there is not a murmur of dissent. When, in 2016, *Investor's Business Daily* dropped cartoons from Mike Ramirez, a two-time Pulitzer Prize-winning cartoonist, nobody complained about any loss

of freedom of the press – they just accepted it as part of the editorial process. As one journalist who was laid off at the same time put it, 'We didn't like it, but we understood . . . It's just the way newspapers work.'

And besides, provided they don't completely flout the most cherished principles of a newspaper, cartoonists still have a lot of political leeway. Editors tend to believe that politicians are fair game, regardless of their political party. According to Christian Adams, 'There seem to be no real limits on how far a cartoonist can go in lampooning a particular lawmaker.' Steve Bell was allowed to mercilessly caricature three prime ministers in three decades: John Major (underpants over trousers), Tony Blair (mad eye and bald patch) and David Cameron (condom on head). All three resented him for it. When Bell repeatedly portrayed John Prescott as a neutered mutt during the Blair years, the deputy prime minister was so offended he actually threatened to headbutt the cartoonist. According to Bell, 'He said to one of my colleagues: "That bloody cartoonist, he's bloody drawing me as a dog. I'm not a fucking dog." When I heard that, I had to carry on doing the dog with renewed vigour.' The trouble for cartoonists today is that many current politicians actually enjoy being mocked.

Steve Bell's depiction of John Prescott as a dog in July 1997.

As the *Sun*'s Steve Bright puts it, 'What we're up against is the mindset of politicians who are almost impossible to offend. As I've heard time and time again from these people, the one thing worse than us drawing them is us not drawing them.'

It's not just political sensibilities that limit what cartoonists can draw. All newspapers are out to make a profit – and so cartoonists must always keep half an eye on how their cartoons will affect their publication's commercial prospects.

The most obvious way this affects cartoonists is through the constant risk of defamation. A libellous cartoon is a quick-fire way to sink a newspaper. In Britain, though, our cartoonists have been fairly lucky. No publication here has ever been successfully sued for libel over a cartoon. This might be because of the inherent ambiguity of cartooning: while words are explicit (and so can be clearly defamatory), an image can be easily misunderstood or misinterpreted. Indeed, some of the most famous cartoonists in British history caused a furore because of the inherent ambiguity of their drawings. The most famous example is probably Philip Zec's wartime cartoon 'The Price of Petrol Has Been Increased by One Penny – Official', which showed a torpedoed sailor clinging to a raft. Zec's intention was to suggest that people use petrol sparingly, as it was costing the lives of merchant seamen to bring it across the Atlantic. But the government thought Zec was accusing them of profiteering from the deaths of seamen ('Worthy of Goebbels,' was how one minister described it).

The plus side of this inherent ambiguity is that it's very rare for cartoonists to find themselves in the dock for defamation. The closest Britain has come to a successful libel case over a cartoon was in 2001–2, when Stagecoach boss Brian Souter launched a claim against Steve Bell for creating a character called Mr Plooker – a bus-driving homophobe – during a row over the repeal of the anti-gay education law Section 28.

Souter said that Bell had based Mr Plooker on him – an allegation Bell did not deny. Souter eventually dropped the action, claiming he had received 'assurances' from the *Guardian* that its team had no intention of suggesting he held extreme views.

There are other, more subtle commercial considerations facing cartoonists. Editors are particularly concerned that cartoonists might offend their advertisers. Steve Bell discovered this the hard way. 'When I unrolled a huge condom on David Cameron the editor hated it,' says Bell. 'The then-editor, Alan Rusbridger, said he didn't want to see any more condoms', because they might offend advertisers. 'We had a terrible toing and froing over several months,' he recalls. However, Rusbridger relented when he discovered that the *Guardian*'s advertisers did not have a problem with a condom-headed PM.

The commercial viability of a newspaper is also dependent on keeping readers on side. And so it is crucial that cartoonists do not publish cartoons that are seen as excessively crass or tasteless by the readership. According to Patrick Blower, 'I do self-censor. I understand the parameters of what the newspaper will publish and submit ideas accordingly. The parameters are unspoken and are mainly dictated by the issue of

The first draft of Patrick Blower's *Telegraph* cartoon on drug use in the Conservative Party. The woman snorting cocaine was subsequently removed.

taste and the emphasis is on restraint.' Scott Clissold of the *Express* has had similar experiences: 'If you send over four ideas on the same topic making the same point, and all of them may be considered offensive by someone, the editor will still run one of them. But it might be the one that contains less nudity, bodily functions, swearing, blood and guts etc.'

Of course, each publication has a different tolerance for 'tasteless' humour. The archly conservative *Telegraph* is rather less au fait with crude jokes than the liberal *Guardian*. 'The fact is the *Telegraph* will simply not publish the kind of cartoons that appear in the *Guardian*, irrespective of political slant,' says Blower. 'It would be an exercise in stupidity to send in drawings showing shit or blood, because they would be rejected every time.' *Telegraph* editors are also less relaxed about things like drugs and sex. For example, during the furore around the then-Tory leadership candidate Michael Gove having taken cocaine in his youth, Blower 'depicted a roomful of stoned Tories smoking hash' but was asked to remove a character snorting cocaine. 'I thought about it for a short while and concluded that amending the cartoon didn't weaken it in any way, in fact it arguably made it lighter and funnier,' Blower recalls.

OF COURSE THERE WILL BE A ROLE FOR THE UN:

Steve Bell removed some of the 'splattered turds' in this cartoon from the version that appeared in print. Online, however, the turds remained in place.

While the left-leaning press tends to be more relaxed, it too has its limits. Some years ago, Steve Bell received a letter from a *Guardian* editor in which he was told the word 'fuck' was banned. The letter concluded with a P.S.: 'The same applies to "cunt".' And in 2003, Bell had to adapt the 'turd count' in a cartoon featuring George W. Bush on the role of the UN. He finally agreed to remove 'three splattered turds' from the version that eventually appeared in the printed version of the *Guardian* – but Bell was pleased that all the turds remained in the version that appeared on their website. A few of Bell's offending cartoons have featured in previous editions of this anthology – such as an image in 2018 that showed the Queen's naked bottom.

Cartoonists feeling restrained by such boringly commercial considerations can take heart from the fact that times do change. According to Christian Adams: 'What is judged taboo or bad taste wafts and waves with time. It used to be considered in bad taste to be insolent to politicians. It used to be taboo to use mild sexual innuendo or mock the Royal Family.' This final taboo was once so serious that cartoonists avoided drawing the royals altogether. David Low drew a rather sympathetic pencil caricature of Edward VIII – then Prince of Wales – in 1928,

David Low's irreverent 1936 cartoon on the difficulty of satirising the Abdication Crisis – it was seen as deeply disrespectful to portray the monarchy.

and was accused of being a 'Bolshevik'. Only in the 1960s did the Royal Family become a regular fixture of political cartoons. This was all to do with keeping readers on side – and so keeping a newspaper's finances afloat.

Usually the political and commercial considerations affecting a cartoonist are fairly predictable. However, there is one area that is much more fraught: when cartoons are at risk of being politically incorrect. Editors and cartoonists often have rather different views of what you can and can't say (or draw).

Cartoonists themselves are split on the value of offensiveness. Some see it as part of their duty.

'A cartoon needs to unsettle and discomfort the reader a little if it is to penetrate the target and not simply bounce off,' says Dave Brown. 'Personally, I've always believed if a political cartoonist is not causing offence then he's just not doing the job right . . . If everybody agrees with what you are saying then you're not saying much at all.' Peter Schrank makes a similar point: 'It's pretty much impossible not to offend, especially in a job where the raison d'être is to poke fun at someone or something. If the object of our ridicule doesn't take offence, then others will do on their behalf.' Some, though, are rather more restrained. According to Peter Brookes, causing offence for the sake of it is 'a mug's game'. You can justify being offensive, but only when it is relevant: 'I want to give offence in the context of what is happening politically on a day-to-day basis,' he says.

The debate about offensiveness has become more loaded in the last few years, arguably thanks to the rise of social media. Many cartoonists think that people are more likely to take offence than they were a few years ago – and when they do, they can easily whip up a storm about it on Twitter. Dave Brown summarises this view: 'Increasingly people seem to believe they have a right not to be offended, and that anything that more than one person finds offensive should be censored, banned, grovellingly apologised for, and the culprit fired,' he says. 'I, on the other hand, believe everybody should be offended at least once a day, preferably by one of my cartoons. It's good to be unsettled, tipped out of our comfort zones and made to think.'

There are a few particular areas where cartoonists are particularly likely to get themselves into hot water. One is in the use of violent imagery. There's nothing worse than a cartoon being construed as endorsing or condoning violence. The associate editor of the *Independent*, Sean O'Grady, is of the opinion that the use of nooses, knives and guns as visual metaphors is in bad taste: 'Drawing politicians stabbing each other in the back during a knife crime epidemic is both odd and wrong,' he says. 'Alternative metaphors are required, otherwise weapons appear gratuitous and frankly worthless.' Steve Bell had two cartoons refused publication soon after the murder of the Labour MP Jo Cox in 2016 on these grounds, as they featured politicians with revolvers. Patrick Blower had similar trouble depicting Theresa May. 'In the darkest days of May's premiership, there was no issue drawing her as an utterly spent force but the *Telegraph* drew the line at any depiction of physical violence towards her, presumably on the

When Peter Brookes drew Pope Benedict XVI with a condom on his head, he received a complaint from the head of the Catholic Church in England and Wales.

grounds that it strays too close to domestic violence against women.'

And that's not to mention religion. Believers taking offence at sacrilegious cartoons is hardly a recent phenomenon. During the 1970s and 1980s, cartoonist Bernard Cookson made fun of both Catholicism and the IRA in his cartoons for the *Express* and *Evening Standard*. The results were terrifying: 'I received a number of telephone calls and letters from the IRA . . . informing me that they knew where I lived and saying they would come and torch my house and family. I took it seriously and so did my editor (they had his address as well!), who asked me to ease up on anti-IRA cartoons, which I did.' Peter Brookes too has had an uncomfortable – albeit less dangerous – experience of mocking Catholicism, in particular Pope Benedict XVI's statement that condoms aggravate the spread of HIV/AIDS. 'I did a cartoon of Pope Benedict XVI with a giant condom on his head. The tip of the condom had a pin through it,' recalls Brookes. 'My cartoon caused an instant storm but I felt strongly that he was talking through his (papal) hat.' The then-leader of the Roman Catholic Church in England and Wales, Cardinal Cormac Murphy-O'Connor, went so far as to organise a meeting of Catholic cardinals with *The Times*. According to Brookes, one person said in the meeting that the pope is infallible. The editor replied, 'That's funny. To us, Peter Brookes is infallible.'

The most fraught issue for cartoonists is race. Along with much of the media, cartooning remains disproportionately white (and male) – a problem that cartoonists are all too aware of. Fortunately, most now put great thought into portraying people of all races with sensitivity, and without invoking harmful stereotypes. As Steve Bell says, 'The fact of drawing, simply copying precisely, or even exaggerating certain physical characteristics of someone of any race, creed or colour does not constitute racism. The intention, meaning and context of the drawing are crucial as to the determination of whether it is racist or not.' However, some cartoonists still struggle to get this balance right. The most recent example was the furore around a cartoon by the Australian artist Mark Knight, who depicted Serena Williams jumping angrily up and down at the US Open. The National Association of Black Journalists in the United States said the cartoon was 'repugnant on many levels', arguing that 'Williams' depiction is unnecessarily sambo-like' – a reference to the 1899 children's book, *The Story of Little Black Sambo*, which features derogatory depictions of black people (Knight responded by saying the cartoon was merely about Williams' 'poor behaviour on the court'). Likewise, in 2013 Gerald Scarfe – then of the *Sunday Times* – faced criticism for portraying Benjamin Netanyahu building a border wall using the blood of Palestinians as cement. His critics said this was a reference to the 'blood libel', the antisemitic myth that Jewish people slaughtered Christian children. Scarfe apologised, but said 'the drawing was a criticism of Netanyahu, and not of the Jewish people: there was no slight whatsoever intended against them.' Again, though, it reveals that cartoonists need

WHY DON'T THEY CRAWL BACK TO WHERE THEY CAME FROM?

Dave Brown thinks the role of cartoonists is to cause offence – not least to politicians, and definitely not least to Donald Trump.

to be hyper-vigilant to the connotations of what they are drawing.

All in all, it seems that cartoonists aren't nearly as independent as they like to think. Between keeping advertisers on side and avoiding undue offence to readers, they have to be just as measured as any journalist. This is inevitable: cartoonists are, at heart, newspaper employees like any other. Nonetheless, we can be sure that cartoonists will continue to push the boundaries of good taste, and in the process challenge their readership and their editors. Dave Brown summarises the approach of the good cartoonist: 'Like the little boy in the Hans Christian Andersen story, unafraid to be thought stupid, the cartoonist is the person who points and says: "The emperor's not wearing any clothes." Though of course, being cartoonists we feel compelled to add: "And he's got a ludicrously small . . .".'

THE CARTOONS

4 September 2018
Ben Jennings
Guardian

Boris Johnson tore into Theresa May's Brexit strategy, saying that Prime Minister Theresa May's strategy would lead to 'victory for the EU'. The statement was Johnson's first intervention on Brexit since quitting the government two months previously, when he had commented that the prime minister was leading Britain to a 'semi-Brexit' that would leave the UK with the 'status of a colony'. Downing Street dismissed Johnson's intervention, with a spokesperson saying that Johnson had 'no new ideas'.

The Labour Party adopted the International Holocaust Remembrance Alliance's definition of antisemitism, following pressure from prominent Labour figures and Jewish groups. The party leadership had originally resisted adopting the definition in full, for fear that it would prevent criticism of Israeli government policies – a decision that sparked heavy criticism from Labour politicians including Chuka Umunna, Gordon Brown, Tony Blair and Margaret Hodge.

5 September 2018
Steve Bell
Guardian

7 September 2018
Peter Brookes
The Times

President Donald Trump came under renewed pressure over his alleged links to the Kremlin, after new information emerged about the assassination attempt on former Russian intelligence agent Sergei Skripal. UK police released information about the two Russian agents they suspected had poisoned Skripal using a fake perfume bottle that contained the nerve agent Novichok. Meanwhile, the *New York Times* printed an article by an anonymous White House official that said the administration was deliberately attempting to curb Trump's powers. The president responded by tweeting 'TREASON?'.

Boris Johnson announced that he had split from his wife of 25 years, the lawyer Marina Wheeler. In a statement to the Press Association, the pair said they had decided several months previously that 'it was in our best interests to separate'. The news came amid rumours that Johnson was poised to make a bid to replace Theresa May as prime minister, following his heavy criticism of her Brexit policy.

7 September 2018
Christian Adams
Evening Standard

According to the cartoonist, 'Former Prime Minister Tony Blair said he was "not sure it was possible" for Labour "moderates" to take the party back from the left, suggesting Labour had been through a "profound change" under Jeremy Corbyn. Continuing his bloody battle with the hard left from the 1990s, Blair hinted at the emergence of a new "progressive, moderate" party. Meanwhile, Vince Cable unveiled plans for the Liberal Democrats to become a "movement for moderates" by opening the leadership vote to non-members. Lib Dem support had dwindled and the party had been struggling electorally since the 2010 coalition with the Tories. Did he still have any friends? Maybe one in the Dear Leader Blair.'

8 September 2018
Andy Davey
Telegraph

Tony Blair's comments about Brexit and the Labour Party led commentators to reflect on the role previous prime ministers had played in causing the current political turmoil. Blair's critics said that the 'dodgy dossier' his government had used to build support for the 2003 invasion of Iraq had caused a collapse in trust in politicians – and that David Cameron's subsequent decision (aided by his coalition partner Nick Clegg) to hold a referendum had brought the problem to a head.

9 September 2018
Chris Riddell
Observer

9 September 2018
Brian Adcock
Independent

The Labour backbencher Chuka Umunna accused Jeremy Corbyn of driving centre-left MPs out of the party. Umunna, a leading member of the cross-party campaign for a second EU referendum, said moderates like himself faced a 'clear and present danger' of being run out of the party by the hard left – especially if local parties began to 'deselect' sitting Labour MPs. Meanwhile, the government announced plans to reform the divorce process, making it easier for couples to break up.

Boris Johnson faced criticism for saying that Theresa May had 'wrapped a suicide vest' around the British constitution and 'handed the detonator' to Brussels. Politicians from across the political spectrum condemned the comments, made in an article in the *Mail on Sunday*, as distasteful. But commentators suggested that the furore would do little to alienate supporters of the politically bulletproof former foreign secretary.

10 September 2018
Steve Bright
Sun

A protestor told the children of the pro-Brexit Tory MP Jacob Rees-Mogg, 'Your daddy is a horrible person,' during a protest outside his house. After a video of the incident circulated on social media, Rees-Mogg brushed it off, saying, 'We are a free country . . . I am in public life and not everybody is going to like me.' Meanwhile, Tory Brexiteers opposed to Theresa May's Brexit plan – including David Davis and Boris Johnson – met to discuss how they could force the prime minister to stand down.

14 September 2018
Peter Brookes
The Times

The two men named as suspects in the poisoning of former Russian spy Sergei Skripal claimed they had been visiting the city as tourists. Alexander Petrov and Ruslan Boshirov told the Russian-state-run channel RT that they had gone to Skripal's hometown because they wanted to see Salisbury Cathedral. 'It's famous for its 123-metre spire,' they said. Intelligence experts continued to speculate that the attempted assassination was ordered by Vladimir Putin's Kremlin.

15 September 2018
Kevin Kallaugher
Economist

Vince Cable, the leader of the Liberal Democrats, used his speech at the party's annual conference to say that Brexit 'can and it must be stopped'. He urged Theresa May and Jeremy Corbyn to get behind the cross-party movement for another referendum, the People's Vote campaign. To Brian Adcock, Cable's comments were reminiscent of an infamous speech by the one-time leader of the Liberal Party, David Steel, who in 1981 told conference delegates to 'go back to your constituencies and prepare for government'. His electoral alliance subsequently won just 11 seats in the 1983 general election.

19 September 2018
Brian Adcock
Independent

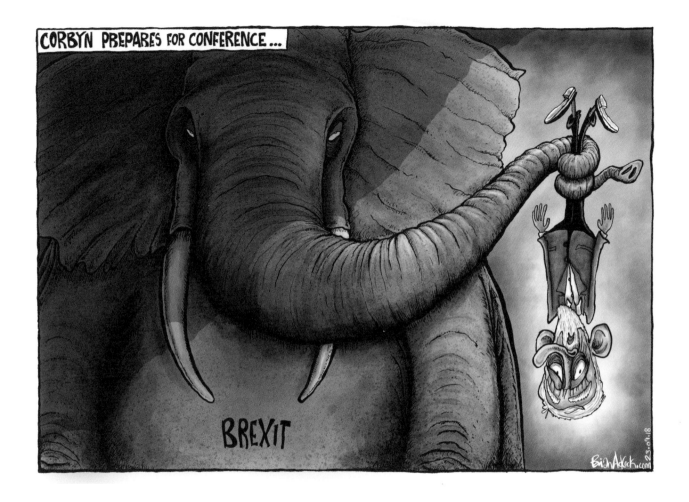

With the Labour conference just days away, the party remained split over whether to back a second referendum on Brexit. While leader Jeremy Corbyn maintained that the 2016 referendum result must be honoured, he was coming under increasing pressure from within his own party to back a People's Vote.

23 September 2018
Brian Adcock
Independent

25 September 2018
Patrick Blower
Daily Telegraph

Critics accused the shadow chancellor, John McDonnell, of wanting to build a Soviet-style economy in the UK, after he announced a string of radical new policies. Announced by McDonnell but backed by Labour leader Jeremy Corbyn and senior figures such as Tom Watson and Keir Starmer, the policies included renationalising the UK's water companies and the creation of a new 'inclusive ownership fund' for businesses.

A series of women made sexual assault allegations against Donald Trump's nominee to join the US Supreme Court, Brett Kavanaugh. According to the cartoonist, 'It looked as if the Democrats were going to make big gains in the mid-terms. The #MeToo campaign was building and Kavanaugh had been accused by at least three women of sexual assault or lewd behaviour in his youth . . . Things had to be done quickly in order to get him sworn in before the Democrats took control of the House, so Trump intervened on his behalf, rubbishing his accusers, and even mocking one at a rally.'

28 September 2018
Andy Davey
Evening Standard

Boris Johnson arrived at the Conservative Party conference in advance of his eagerly anticipated speech to members. Commentators speculated that he would use his speech to try to outmanoeuvre Theresa May, in order to replace her as prime minister. Earlier in the week, Johnson had been photographed running through a wheat field – widely interpreted as a mocking reference to May's famous statement that 'running through fields of wheat' was the naughtiest thing she had ever done.

2 October 2018
Christian Adams
Evening Standard

"SHUT UP! GO AWAY!!"

4297·5·10·18 – Belltoons.co.uk –   – ©Steve Bell 2018 –   AFTER LOW

The defence minister, Gavin Williamson, condemned Russia as a 'pariah state' in the wake of allegations that the Kremlin had attempted to hack the Foreign Office. The comments were the latest in a string of attacks on Vladimir Putin's regime: Williamson had previously said that Russia should 'go away and shut up'. To Steve Bell, the whole incident reminded him of a famous David Low cartoon from the Second World War. In the original, published in 1940, a British soldier stands at the coast waving his fist at oncoming Luftwaffe planes, with the caption 'Very well, alone'.

5 October 2018
Steve Bell
Guardian

Investigative journalists uncovered the identities of several hundred Kremlin spies, in the latest setback for the Russian spy agency GRU. The online news outfit *Bellingcat* discovered the names, number plates and passport details of 305 espionage agents in a public online database – leading to allegations that Vladimir Putin's secret service had lost the plot. The artist Banksy, meanwhile, hit the headlines after building a secret shredder into one of his artworks. The painting destroyed itself seconds after it was bought at an auction for £860,000.

7 October 2018
Scott Clissold
Sunday Express

Theresa May walked on stage at the Conservative Party conference to the Abba song 'Dancing Queen', a reference to a viral video of her dancing awkwardly on a trade visit to South Africa. But critics said that her humorous entrance was a distraction from her beleaguered Brexit policy, and her party's dependency on the DUP and its leader, Arlene Foster. 'Cartoonists and satirists are always grateful when someone in the public eye sticks their neck out and risks looking foolish,' says the cartoonist. 'But by the time she danced to the lectern at the Tory Party conference it was clear that her PR team were now in charge. She'd probably been coached by a professional. Not that it improved her performance.'

7 October 2018
Peter Schrank
Sunday Business Post

10 October 2018
Patrick Blower
Daily Telegraph

Nicola Sturgeon used her speech at the Scottish National Party conference to argue that Brexit would make independence more likely. 'Brexit is about turning inwards,' she said. 'Independence is about being open, outward-looking, aspiring to play our full part in the world around us.' But Brexiteers took to social media to suggest that Scotland couldn't be truly independent until it left the EU.

'Nowadays, Sir, it's very important to get an acceptable inscription on the cake. So how about: 'Should've gone to Specsavers?'

The Supreme Court ruled that a Northern Irish bakery did not break the law when its Christian owners refused to decorate a cake with the slogan 'Support Gay Marriage'. The court ruled that the Ashers Bakery had rejected the order because they did not support the message on the cake – rather than because of the sexuality of the man who placed the order – and so their decision was not discriminatory.

11 October 2018
Stan McMurtry
Daily Mail

The work and pensions secretary, Esther McVey, acknowledged that some people would be worse off as a result of the government's reforms to the benefits system – but said that the most vulnerable would be protected. In response to reports that 3.2 million households would lose more than £2,000 a year, McVey maintained that the new Universal Credit payment would be 'much better than the old system'. McVey's opponents said it strengthened her reputation as an uncaring benefits minister – or, in Dave Brown's view, as a latter-day Cruella de Vil.

12 October 2018
Dave Brown
Independent

As the Queen's granddaughter, Prince Eugenie, tied the knot in Windsor, the government hinted at new plans to win the Democratic Unionist Party round to the controversial northern Irish backstop. Newspapers reported that Theresa May intended to extend the transition period of Brexit – which would ensure that the backstop would never come into place. Critics of the prime minister said that she had already made enough concessions to the DUP, not least the £1 billion she offered Arlene Foster's party in the wake of the 2017 general election.

13 October 2018
Martin Rowson
Guardian

14 October 2018
Chris Riddell
Observer

Theresa May declared that the government's eight-year programme of austerity was 'over'. The prime minister used her Conservative Party conference speech to tell the public that there are 'better days ahead', and that the government would increase investment in public services. But critics said that her optimistic speech was misleading, considering her administration's continued problems with its Universal Credit benefits reform, its relationship with the DUP, and, above all, with Brexit.

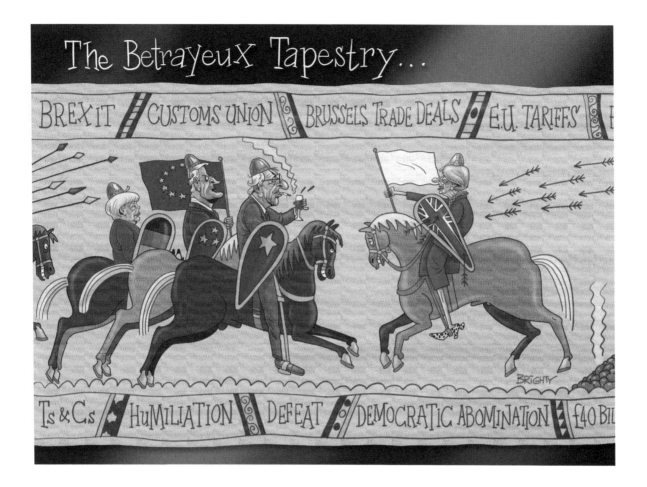

Criticism of Theresa May's Brexit strategy intensified in the days after her Conservative Party conference speech. Writing in the *Sun*, columnist Trevor Kavanaugh said, 'Unless stopped by her cabinet, her MPs or by parliament itself, this prime minister seems to be leading us to the greatest defeat since the Norman Conquest in 1066' – an image memorably illustrated in this recreation of the Bayeux Tapestry, featuring May and EU leaders Angela Merkel, Michel Barnier and Jean-Claude Juncker.

15 October 2018
Steve Bright
Sun

17 October 2018
Dave Brown
Independent

Eight cabinet ministers held a secret meeting to plot their opposition to a soft Brexit. The gathering – which was attended by politicians including Michael Gove, Chris Grayling and Jeremy Hunt – was christened the 'pizza cabinet', because of the food the politicians shared as they discussed their plans. Theresa May's supporters said that the meeting was not really about Brexit, and was instead to do with the ambition of political figures who would profit from her downfall.

Protesters seeking a referendum on the final Brexit deal attended a rally in London. The People's Vote campaign, which organised the march, said that around 700,000 people had attended – making it the largest demonstration for a second referendum yet. Meanwhile, Theresa May returned from the latest round of increasingly fraught discussions with the EU.

21 October 2018
Brian Adcock
Independent

Donald Trump announced that the United States was withdrawing from a key nuclear weapons treaty with Russia. Trump told reporters that Russia had 'violated' the 1987 Intermediate-Range Nuclear Forces treaty, and that the White House would not let the Kremlin 'go out and do weapons [when] we're not allowed to'. In other news, the porn actress Stormy Daniels – who says that she had an affair with Trump in 2006 – released her autobiography, *Full Disclosure*. The book described Trump's 'unusual penis', which has a 'huge mushroom head. Like a toadstool.'

22 October 2018
Ben Jennings
Guardian

The Crown Prince of Saudi Arabia, Prince Mohammad bin Salman, denied any involvement in the death of the journalist Jamal Khashoggi, a prominent critic of his regime. Khashoggi had been murdered and dismembered while inside the Saudi consulate in Istanbul three weeks previously.

23 October 2018
Dave Brown
Independent

27 October 2018
Martin Rowson
Guardian

The retail entrepreneur Philip Green was named in Parliament as the man accused by a newspaper of sexual harassment. The *Telegraph* had previously reported the allegations, but, due to an injunction, had not been able to name Green. However, the Labour peer Peter Hain used parliamentary privilege to publicly name the Topshop boss. Green 'categorically and wholly' denied the allegations.

'After months of tension between Downing Street and the Treasury over the extent to which the Tories should respond to Jeremy Corbyn's policies, the chancellor was forced to ditch his pro-austerity stance in the autumn budget,' says the cartoonist. 'Hammond announced that local councils in England would get an extra £420 million to tackle a growing number of potholes, alongside a £28.8 billion fund to upgrade England's motorways. This was seen as a reputational sop to Theresa May, whose fortunes appeared to be sagging.'

29 October 2018
Andy Davey
Telegraph

The entrepreneur and pro-Brexit campaigner Arron Banks was referred to the National Crime Agency over 'multiple suspected offences'. Banks was one of the key funders of the Leave.EU campaign in the run-up to the EU referendum, which some journalists had suggested was linked with Vladimir Putin's Kremlin. But Banks said he welcomed the development, saying, 'I am confident that a full and frank investigation will finally put an end to the ludicrous allegations levelled against me and my colleagues.'

1 November 2018
Morten Morland
The Times

David Cameron told friends that he had been 'bored shitless' since stepping back from front-line politics. The *Sun* reported that Cameron was hoping for a spell as foreign secretary, quoting a source who said, 'He is still a young man.' But commentators suggested that the last thing the beleaguered prime minister would want was the advice of her predecessor. 'Old foes popping back – that's always a joy,' says the cartoonist. 'It feels like revisiting an old friend. And no need to get out the reference pictures. We know how to draw them by heart.'

4 November 2018
Peter Schrank
Sunday Times

Woman in record-breaking attempt to cross the whole of Westminster before the bell tolls...

6 November 2018
Morten Morland
The Times

Theresa May rejected calls to resign or abandon her Brexit strategy, saying that a change of course would lead to 'deep and grave uncertainty' for the future of the country. Meanwhile, the grandson of Florence Ilott, a British amateur sprinter, paid tribute to his 'remarkable' grandmother's record-breaking sprint across Westminster Bridge in 1934. She was the first person to complete the run in the time it took for Big Ben to chime 12 noon.

Prince Charles said he would stop campaigning on controversial topics when he becomes king. The heir to the throne is famous for his interventions on subjects ranging from architecture to the environment. But he told the BBC it was 'nonsense' to suggest that he would continue to make such comments as monarch. He also revealed that he frequently speaks to plants, saying, 'I happily talk to the plants and the trees, and listen to them. I think it's absolutely crucial.'

8 November 2018
Christian Adams
Evening Standard

8 November 2018
Steve Bell
Guardian

The Republican Party had a mixed night at the US mid-term elections. Donald Trump described his party's results as a 'tremendous success', after Republicans gained two seats in the Senate, pointing out that governing parties rarely win seats at such elections. However, the Democrats gained control of the House of Representatives, winning 41 seats from their opponents.

"Well, if you knows of a better 'ole, go to it."

Theresa May's Brexit strategy suffered a further setback after her minister of transport resigned from the government. Jo Johnson – the brother of Boris – demanded a second referendum on leaving the EU, and said that May's approach was a 'con'. His comments were only the latest in a string of attacks on the prime minister's approach, coming from politicians including Jacob Rees-Mogg, Boris Johnson and David Davis. However, Tory grandees such as Philip Hammond and Michael Gove continued to support the prime minister. Peter Brookes' cartoon is a pastiche of a classic wartime cartoon of 1915, by Bruce Bairnsfather.

10 November 2018
Peter Brookes
The Times

12 November 2018
Ben Jennings
Guardian

Donald Trump came under fire for joking about the bad weather during his speech at an Armistice Day event. While attending a memorial ceremony in Paris, attended by his wife Melania as well as German premier Angela Merkel, he turned to a group of Second World War veterans and said, 'You look so comfortable up there, under shelter, as we're getting drenched.' It was not the first time the president had been criticised for disrespecting war veterans. In 2015, he controversially said of the Arizona politician and veteran John McCain, 'He's a "war hero" because he was captured [whereas] I like people who weren't captured.'

Jacob Rees-Mogg called for a vote of no confidence in Theresa May, sparking speculation that a crucial poll on her premiership was imminent. The Brexiteer MP wrote to the chair of the Tory backbench 1922 Committee calling for the vote, saying that she had broken her own red lines on Brexit. In other news, the iconic David Hockney painting *Portrait of an Artist (Pool with Two Figures)* – masterfully recreated here by Christian Adams – sold for £70.2 million, a record sum for a work of art by a living artist.

16 November 2018
Christian Adams
Evening Standard

Theresa May said she was committed to leaving the EU in March, in spite of growing criticism of her Brexit deal from within her own party. She brushed off speculation about a vote of no confidence in her premiership, saying, 'Am I going to see this through? Yes.' According to the cartoonist, 'When I drew this, I felt a certain amount of sympathy for Theresa May. But in this instance I was wrong: May has since proved that she is catastrophically incompetent and therefore deserving of the harshest criticism.' He also reflects on the changing significance of the White Cliffs of Dover in cartoons: 'Before Brexit they had been associated with the Blitz spirit and a kind of hopeful yearning for the safety of home soil; now they represent a place of danger, a rift with the continent.'

16 November 2018
Peter Schrank
Guardian

THANKSNOTGIVING DAY...

GO HOME

MIGRANT CARAVAN

Donald Trump threatened to shut down the border with Mexico. As a caravan of thousands of migrants from South America tried to reach the US, the president described it as 'a really bad situation', saying he was tempted to 'close entry into the country for a period of time until we can get it under control'. Liberal journalists said that the president's comments were particularly harsh coming just days before the Thanksgiving national holiday.

22 November 2018
David Simonds
Evening Standard

SUPPORT MY DEAL – OR ELSE!

24 November 2018
Ben Jennings
i

Theresa May warned the House of Commons that if they didn't vote for her Brexit deal they risked having 'no Brexit at all'. Describing her settlement as 'the best that could be negotiated', she told MPs that the alternatives were to crash out with no-deal or to remain in the EU. But commentators said that May's intransigent approach was unlikely to win round backbench Tory MPs, and would only hurt her prospects.

Jacob Rees-Mogg's attempt to remove Theresa May as prime minister stalled. Along with other pro-Brexit MPs – possibly including Boris Johnson and David Davis – the Tory MP had written a letter formally requesting a vote of no confidence in the Conservative leader. But as the week wore on, it became apparent that not enough MPs had advocated such a vote for one to be held. As the coup attempt descended into farce, Rees-Mogg admitted to being a fan of *Dad's Army*, saying, 'I've always admired Captain Mainwaring.'

24 November 2018
Graeme Bandeira
Yorkshire Post

DONALD TRUMPINGTON...

ANGLO-US TRADE DEAL

28 November 2018
Peter Brookes
The Times

The former Tory peer Baroness Trumpington died at the age of 96. Known for her irreverent sense of humour, Trumpington had hit the headlines in 2012 for sticking two fingers up at a colleague in the House of Lords after he made a comment about her age. Donald Trump, meanwhile, dashed Theresa May's hopes of a post-Brexit trade deal, warning that the UK 'may not be able to trade with the US' if it accepted her deal with the EU.

The government published an analysis of the long-term economic effects of Brexit, calculating that all possible outcomes would leave Britain worse off. Later that day, the Bank of England warned that a no-deal Brexit would cause a crash in the value of the pound, with GDP also falling by up to 8 per cent. Commentators reacted with dismay to the predictions, with ITV's Joel Hills describing them as 'borderline apocalyptic'.

29 November 2018
Dave Brown
Independent

3 December 2018
Christian Adams
Evening Standard

Theresa May and Jeremy Corbyn agreed to debate one another on Brexit on live television. But the planned debate, suggested by the prime minister as part of her attempts to gain support for her deal, came under fire from smaller parties. The Liberal Democrats, the SNP and the Greens all argued that they should be included, because the two main parties only represented a narrow range of opinions on Brexit.

'Oh dear. Your depression has gone but your blood pressure's zoomed upwards again, Mr Wagstaff'

The *Daily Mail* launched a Christmas campaign inviting readers to volunteer at their local hospitals. The newspaper asked volunteers to help the NHS by befriending patients, collecting prescriptions and assisting at mealtimes. Theresa May backed the campaign, calling on people to offer 'companionship and support' to those in need.

4 December 2018
Stan McMurtry
Daily Mail

MPs found Theresa May's government to be in contempt of parliament. The government had failed to publish the full legal advice on her Brexit deal, in spite of an earlier vote in the House of Commons calling on it to do so. As a result, MPs voted to castigate the government for ignoring its wishes. May accused Labour of 'playing parlour games', while her backers said that the general public was bored of Brexit and wanted Labour to let the government get on with it.

5 December 2018
Patrick Blower
Telegraph

The atmosphere in parliament became increasingly febrile after a number of pro-Brexit politicians renewed their attacks on the prime minister's deal. Amid growing criticism of May from the likes of Jacob Rees-Mogg, Boris Johnson and David Davis, the DUP leader Arlene Foster tweeted that the withdrawal agreement was 'fundamentally flawed'. Meanwhile, 'yellow vest' activists assembled in Paris for their latest round of protests – and possibly riots – in response to the French government's policies.

8 December 2018
Peter Brookes
The Times

9 December 2018
Brian Adcock
Independent

With Theresa May's deal looking diminishingly likely to get through parliament, the backbencher Amber Rudd suggested a Norway-style arrangement with the EU as a possible alternative. Rudd said that if May's deal were voted down, she would advocate an agreement that involved staying part of the European Economic Area. But her critics suggested that this was even more of a dead parrot than May's deal, and even Rudd acknowledged 'nobody knows if it can be done'.

With the indefatigability of a Duracell bunny, Theresa May continued on her tour around the UK, attempting to muster up support for her Brexit deal. But as her relationship with her parliamentary colleagues became increasingly frayed, the future of May's agreement looked ever less certain. Over the weekend, cabinet ministers warned the prime minister that if her deal failed to pass, she would have to step down.

9 December 2018
Morten Morland
The Times

Theresa May called off a crucial House of Commons vote on her Brexit deal, the day before it was scheduled to take place. Despite having spent the last month trying to rally support for her deal, the prime minister acknowledged that parliament would still have rejected it 'by a significant margin'. With May's position looking increasingly untenable, a gloomy photo of the prime minister in the rain captured the mood of her increasingly beleaguered premiership – and inspired Dave Brown to produce the above cartoon.

11 December 2018
Dave Brown
Independent

Theresa May won a vote of confidence held by Conservative MPs. The secret ballot was triggered after 48 MPs wrote letters to the chair of the Tory backbench 1922 Committee, saying they no longer had faith in the prime minister's leadership. Meanwhile, the Disney film *Mary Poppins Returns* opened in cinemas.

13 December 2018
Peter Brookes
The Times

CHAIN OF COMMAND

15 December 2018
Ingram Pinn
Financial Times

Michael Cohen, the former 'fixer' to President Donald Trump, was sentenced to three years in prison for fraud and campaign finance violations committed during the 2016 presidential election campaign. Cohen's crimes came to light during an investigation into Russian interference in US politics by Robert Mueller. Cohen had pleaded guilty to the crimes, but said that he was merely following commands from the president himself. 'Nothing at the Trump organisation was ever done unless it was run through Mr Trump,' he told journalists.

Theresa May was caught on camera having an argument with Jean-Claude Juncker, the president of the European Commission. In footage shot at a meeting between UK and EU officials in Brussels, May apparently took Juncker to task for criticising her approach to Brexit, asking, 'What did you call me? You called me nebulous.' May later said the pair had had a 'robust discussion', but that her plan to seek 'further clarification and discussion' from the EU was still on track.

16 December 2018
Scott Clissold
Sunday Express

20 December 2018
Steve Bell
Guardian

Jeremy Corbyn denied calling Theresa May a 'stupid woman' during a House of Commons debate. In a widely shared video, the Labour leader seemed to mutter the phrase in the midst of Prime Minister's Questions. But Corbyn claimed he had actually said 'stupid people'. The pair had come to blows after May accused Labour of equivocating over whether to submit a vote of no confidence in the government. 'I know it's the pantomime season, but is he going to put a confidence vote? Oh yes he is,' said the prime minister, prompting Tory MPs to respond, 'Oh no he isn't!'

Gatwick Airport grounded all flights for three days running, after two drones were spotted flying near its runways. Managers called in the police and the military to help identify the operator of the drones, which ultimately caused around 1,000 flights to be diverted or cancelled. Commentators were quick to seize upon the parallels between the grounded flights and the state of Britain's public sector, increasingly immobilised by the turmoil around Brexit.

20 December 2018
Christian Adams
Evening Standard

21 December 2018
Steve Bell
Guardian

A homeless man became the second person in 2018 to die immediately outside the Houses of Parliament. The incident sparked condemnation of the government's failure to tackle homelessness in the UK. In August, Theresa May had outlined a £100 million fund to eradicate street sleeping by 2027. But critics pointed out that over the previous five years, successive governments had presided over a 24 per cent spike in rough-sleeper deaths.

'Oh, come on, Mac! You're supposed to walk happily into the sunset.'

This was the final cartoon by Stan McMurtry – or Mac – for the *Daily Mail*. His retirement came at the end of 50 years at the paper. He said, 'It has been a wonderful 50 years. Full of challenges, remarkable stories, fun and laughter. So what have I learnt? That older people are much easier to draw: more lines, fewer teeth! Golda Meir, the former Israeli prime minister, was a good example, and Donald Trump was a gift from heaven for cartoonists.'

21 December 2018
Stan McMurtry
Daily Mail

VLAD THE IMPECUNIOUS

22 December 2018
Dave Brown
Independent

Vladimir Putin dismissed the possibility of a second referendum on leaving the EU. 'The referendum was held. What can [Theresa May] do? She has to fulfil the will of the people expressed in the referendum,' he said. Remain campaigners said that his intervention was unwelcome, especially considering the Kremlin had allegedly attempted to swing the result in Leave's favour using dirty money.

'Jeremy Corbyn faced a backlash from Labour party members and young voters who felt betrayed over his Brexit stance, or what they understood of it,' says the cartoonist. 'He seemed determined to "honour" Brexit, even though the majority of Labour voters and the overwhelming majority of party members apparently wanted to remain. There were no gifts this Christmas for them. His strategy director, the mean-spirited Trotskyite elf Seumas Milne, dispatched an empty sack to the children.'

24 December 2018
Andy Davey
Independent

The Queen used her Christmas message to offer a veiled comment on Brexit chaos, saying that the call for 'peace on Earth' is 'needed as much as ever'. In a broadcast from Buckingham Palace, she said, 'Even with the most deeply held differences, treating the other person with respect and as a fellow human being is always a good first step towards greater understanding.' Meanwhile, Theresa May retired to her constituency home in Maidenhead for a welcome break from Brexit turmoil.

25 December 2018
Brian Adcock
Independent

Home Secretary Sajid Javid declared a 'major incident' following a spike in the number of migrants illegally attempting to cross the English Channel. According to the cartoonist, 'I enjoy working during the Christmas/New Year period because it usually gives me a chance to get away from daily politics. And I enjoy quoting from the Bible. Along with the work of Shakespeare and the ancient myths, particularly the Greek ones, it has given us a shared trove of stories which can be quoted from and which should be universally understood.'

27 December 2018
Peter Schrank
Guardian

Sajid Javid entered talks with the French government about sending migrants who crossed the English Channel back to France. Labour said Javid was taking 'overblown' action over migrants in order to win round Conservative members, in advance of a leadership bid. In other news, the British Army unveiled its latest recruitment campaign – a series of adverts based on an iconic World War One poster saying 'Your Country Needs YOU' – which it said were aimed at 'snowflakes', 'millennials' and 'selfie addicts'.

3 January 2019
Christian Adams
Evening Standard

A Northern Irish couple won £114 million in a bumper EuroMillions draw. Patrick and Frances Connolly from Moira, County Armagh, said they intended to give a significant portion of their winnings to friends, family and charity. Meanwhile, with speculation intensifying that Theresa May's Brexit deal would be rejected by parliament, economists tried to calculate how much money a no-deal exit would cost the UK.

5 January 2019
Ben Jennings
i

65

Theresa May stood by her transport secretary, Chris Grayling, after the collapse of a disastrous contract with a ferry company. Grayling had come under fire for awarding a £13.8 million Channel ferry contract to an organisation that did not own any ships. The news came just weeks after a scathing report by MPs on Grayling's mismanagement of train timetable changes, which had caused chaos on Britain's railways in May 2018.

6 January 2019
Chris Riddell
Observer

As parliament returned from the Christmas recess, speculation grew that Theresa May's Brexit deal was going to be rejected by MPs. The prime minister insisted that a vote on her settlement would go ahead on 15 January, even though dozens of Tory MPs had said that they would not back it.

7 January 2019
Nicola Jennings
Guardian

9 January 2019
Peter Brookes
The Times

The Remainer Tory MP Anna Soubry was verbally abused while being interviewed outside parliament. Pro-Brexit activists chanted 'Anna Soubry is a Nazi' during a live broadcast on BBC News. Soubry called for the protestors to be prosecuted under public order laws, saying that it was 'astonishing' that 'this is what has happened to our country'.

The speaker of the House of Commons, John Bercow, unexpectedly allowed a vote on an amendment that gave parliament greater control over Brexit. The amendment, proposed by Dominic Grieve, obliged the government to debate its strategy in the House of Commons within days of losing a Brexit vote. Pro-Leave MPs said that Bercow was forcing Theresa May to bend her policies to his will – an idea rather surreally captured in this Steve Bell cartoon.

10 January 2019
Steve Bell
Guardian

REACHING OUT ...

18 January 2019
Dave Brown
Independent

Theresa May suffered a record-breaking defeat on her Brexit plans, losing the parliamentary vote on her deal by a majority of 230. In the wake of her defeat, she called for opposition parties to 'put self-interest aside' and negotiate with her on reaching a deal – a comment widely interpreted as a dig at Jeremy Corbyn's Labour.

Theresa May narrowly won a vote of confidence in the House of Commons. Labour leader Jeremy Corbyn had tabled a motion calling on her to stand down in the wake of the defeat of her Brexit deal – but the prime minister won it by 325 votes to 306. Days earlier, the Duke of Edinburgh had been involved in a car crash while driving near Sandringham. The incident led to calls for the 97-year-old to stop driving.

18 January 2019
Ben Jennings
i

As the fallout continued from the disastrous vote on her EU deal, the prime minister reiterated her commitment to delivering Brexit. Theresa May told MPs she would 'continue to work . . . to deliver on the result of the referendum'. To some, May's unwavering commitment to her deal was reminiscent of an infamous press conference during the 2017 general election. 'Nothing has changed,' she said, moments after announcing a U-turn on her social care policy.

20 January 2019
Morten Morland
The Times

James Dyson, the inventor behind the eponymous vacuum cleaner brand, announced that he was relocating his company to Singapore. One of the Brexit campaign's most ardent supporters, Dyson insisted that the move had nothing to do with the UK's departure from the EU, attributing the decision to the 'increasing majority' of his customers being in Asia.

23 January 2019
Christian Adams
Evening Standard

The Queen urged people to act respectfully and to compromise with one another, in comments widely interpreted as a comment on Brexit. In a speech at the Norfolk Women's Institute, she spoke in favour of 'coming together to seek out the common ground; and never losing sight of the bigger picture'. Critics said that it was not the monarch's place to comment on politics – especially just weeks after the row about Prince Philip's car crash at Sandringham.

26 January 2019
Peter Brookes
The Times

The backbench Labour MP Yvette Cooper put forward a parliamentary amendment that would prevent Britain leaving the EU without a deal. The amendment would have obliged the government to postpone Brexit – then scheduled for 29 March – if Theresa May's deal had not received parliamentary approval by late February. Some commentators pointed out that the amendment fulfilled a similar role to the backstop in the government's existing deal – which Cooper had repeatedly voted against.

29 January 2019
Morten Morland
The Times

31 January 2019
Steve Bell
Guardian

Jeremy Corbyn agreed to face-to-face talks with Theresa May over Brexit. The leader of the opposition had previously rejected calls from the government to collaborate until the prime minister ruled out no-deal. But he changed tack after Labour narrowly lost a series of Brexit votes in the House of Commons.

With Brexit day trundling ever closer, senior cabinet ministers began to speculate that it would have to be delayed. The home secretary, Sajid Javid, reportedly told fellow ministers that he thought Theresa May would run out of time to pass the legislation necessary to leave on 25 March. But polling showed that Britons were ever-more uninterested in Brexit, to such an extent that the media identified a new social group, the 'Bobs' – those 'bored of Brexit'.

2 February 2019
Martin Rowson
Guardian

2 February 2019
Kevin Kallaugher
Economist

Theresa May prepared for new talks with the EU, in which she would ask them to scrap the controversial Northern Ireland backstop. But the president of the European Commission, Jean-Claude Juncker, said that the deal had already been agreed. 'The agreement will not be renegotiated,' he said. 'Ireland's border is Europe's border and it's our union's priority.'

As Theresa May returned to Brussels for further discussions with the EU, her domestic policy agenda received a blow after Nissan cancelled its plans to make a new model of car in Britain. The news was especially damaging because in 2016 May had pointed to the company's presence as proof that manufacturers had faith in post-Brexit Britain.

4 February 2019
Brian Adcock
Independent

FOR THE FEW, NOT THE MANY

Blower 5·2·19

5 February 2019
Patrick Blower
Telegraph

Jeremy Corbyn came under fire for failing to condemn Venezuelan president Nicolás Maduro. The South American state was in the throes of a political crisis, after its government refused to hold fresh elections in spite of international pressure. But the Labour leader said that he opposed any 'interference' in Venezuelan politics, leading to allegations that he was blinded by his support for the left-wing principles of Maduro's regime.

The leader of the DUP, Arlene Foster, denounced the Irish backstop – a crucial part of Theresa May's Brexit deal – as 'toxic'. She said that the backstop threatened the integrity of the union, and that her party would never vote for any agreement that included it. Commentators said that Foster's hard-line stance made it supremely unlikely that May's agreement would pass through parliament.

6 February 2019
Dave Brown
Independent

A SPECIAL PLACE IN HELL

9 February 2019
Ingram Pinn
Financial Times

Donald Tusk, president of the European Council, said that there was a 'special place in hell' for those who had 'promoted Brexit without even a sketch of a plan of how to carry it'. Although Tusk didn't name specific politicians (or specific statements) his comments were widely interpreted as an attack on Leave campaigners such as Boris Johnson, Michael Gove, Liam Fox, Jacob Rees-Mogg and David Davis – and especially their questionable campaign promise to secure £350 million extra for the NHS if Britain left the EU.

Labour MP Luciana Berger faced a no-confidence vote in her Liverpool constituency, sparking new allegations of antisemitism in the party. Berger's critics were accused of racism after branding Berger, who is Jewish, as a 'disruptive Zionist'. Berger said that she was being targeted because she had criticised the Labour leader, Jeremy Corbyn, and the shadow chancellor, John McDonnell, for failing to root out antisemitism in the party membership.

12 February 2019
Morten Morland
The Times

14 February 2019
Christian Adams
Evening Standard

John McDonnell came under fire for describing Winston Churchill as a 'villain'. Asked during an interview whether the wartime leader was 'hero or villain', McDonnell responded 'Tonypandy: villain' – a reference to Churchill's notorious 1910 decision to send in the military against rioting miners in Tonypandy, South Wales. Churchill's grandson, the Tory MP Nicholas Soames, said, 'I think my grandfather's reputation can withstand a publicity-seeking assault from a third-rate, Poundland Lenin.'

"ACTIONS HAVE CONSEQUENCES"
GOVERNMENT MINISTER

A government minister said he would not put British troops at risk in order to save a teen-ager who had run away to Syria to join Islamic State. Ben Wallace, the security minister, said that Shamina Begum – who was 15 at the time she joined the terrorist group – should realise that 'actions have consequences'. In an interview with *The Times*, Begum had said that she wanted to 'return home to Britain'. Meanwhile, in the UK, Theresa May suffered another humiliating defeat in the House of Commons over her Brexit strategy.

15 February 2019
Steve Bell
Guardian

16 February 2019
Brian Adcock
i

Senior Democrat Nancy Pelosi vowed that there would not be another government shutdown over Donald Trump's controversial Mexican border policy. The US government had closed down in December and January after Congress refused to fund Trump's plan to build a wall along the US's southern border. The president had repeatedly vowed to declare a national emergency in order to secure funding for the proposal.

Pupils across the UK walked out of their classrooms as part of a global protest about climate change. The 'school strike' took place in more than 60 towns across the UK, with an estimated 15,000 students calling for immediate radical action to save the environment.

16 February 2019
Ben Jennings
i

19 February 2019
Dave Brown
Independent

Seven MPs resigned from the Labour Party to form a new centrist political bloc, The Independent Group. The politicians – Gavin Shuker, Ann Coffey, Angela Smith, Chris Leslie, Mike Gapes, Luciana Berger and Chuka Umunna – had been some of the most prominent critics of Jeremy Corbyn's leadership. The Labour leader said he was 'disappointed' by the decision.

Three MPs resigned from the Conservative Party to join The Independent Group. Anna Soubry, Sarah Wollaston and Heidi Allen had all consistently criticised Theresa May for supporting a hard Brexit. In the press conference after they joined the new grouping, they attacked the government for letting the 'hard-line anti-EU awkward squad' take over the party. But critics asked how much they had in common politically with the existing seven Independent Group MPs, all of whom had joined from the Labour Party.

21 February 2019
Steve Bell
Guardian

THE HOLY SEE

23 February 2019
Nicola Jennings
Guardian

Pope Francis caused outrage among survivors of clerical sexual abuse by giving a 'defensive' speech. Activists had hoped that Francis would use his address to a summit at the Vatican to outline a zero-tolerance approach to paedophile priests. However, instead the pope drew attention to the prevalence of abuse outside of the church, saying perpetrators were 'primarily parents, relatives, husbands of child brides and teachers'.

Footage circulated on social media that showed Theresa May unsuccessfully attempting to play pool with the Italian prime minister, Giuseppe Conte. The video came out as rumours circulated that the prime minister was considering delaying Brexit, in order to increase the chance of her EU deal getting through parliament.

26 February 2019
Patrick Blower
Telegraph

27 February 2019
Christian Adams
Evening Standard

Donald Trump and Kim Jong-un held a historic summit in Hanoi. During the meeting – the second ever between an American president and a North Korean supreme leader – the pair discussed denuclearisation, with Trump hailing Kim as a 'great leader'. Meanwhile, back in the US, the president's former lawyer Michael Cohen delivered an explosive public testimony about his former boss, saying, 'He is a racist, he is a conman, he is a cheat.'

The summit between Donald Trump and Kim Jong-un ended without agreement. Trump said that Kim had demanded that all sanctions be immediately lifted, and that he told the North Korea leader, 'we couldn't do that.' The failure to reach as an agreement was widely interpreted as a blow to Trump's international authority.

28 February 2019
Dave Brown
Independent

1 March 2019
Peter Brookes
The Times

Tom Watson, the deputy Labour leader, criticised Jeremy Corbyn's leadership. He said that Luciana Berger's decision to quit the party over antisemitism was the 'worst day of shame' in Labour's history, and also said that Corbyn still 'has to convince the British public' that he was fit to be prime minister. On the same day, Watson outlined Labour's new policy on gambling, which involved a crackdown on online casinos.

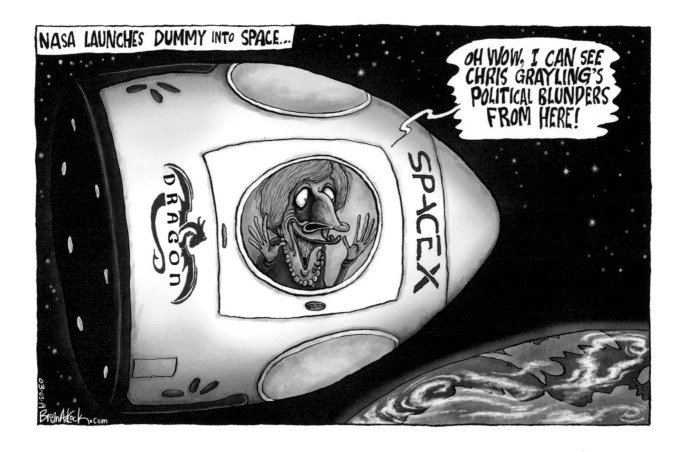

The Labour Party accused the transport secretary, Chris Grayling, of 'serial failure and routine incompetence', after the government agreed to pay out £33 million to settle a dispute over ferries. Eurotunnel had taken legal action after Theresa May's government awarded a lucrative Channel ferry contract to a company that did not own any boats. Meanwhile, Elon Musk's space exploration company, SpaceX, launched a rocket out of the Earth's atmosphere in partnership with NASA.

3 March 2019
Brian Adcock
Independent

5 March 2019
Dave Brown
Independent

Theresa May attempted to lure Labour MPs into voting for her Brexit deal by offering a £1.6 billion investment fund to boost economic growth in Britain's 'left behind' towns. The majority of the fund would have gone to Labour's heartlands in the Midlands and the north of England. Government sources said they hoped the move would win over 20 to 30 opposition MPs, but Labour described the policy as a 'desperate bribe'.

Experts warned that young people had been pushed into violence by austerity. Funding for youth services had been cut by around a third since 2010, leading to the closure of hundreds of youth clubs. 'You have teenagers with no access to services, and there are very few police out, so by definition, kids are going to get up to things,' said Eddie O'Hara, a social worker in Birmingham.

6 March 2019
Ben Jennings
i

9 March 2019
Andy Davey
Telegraph

With Brexit just weeks away, the attorney general, Geoffrey Cox, began work on a legally binding addition to Theresa May's deal that would solve the Irish backstop problem. According to the cartoonist, 'Geoffrey Cox referred rather proudly to the way in which Tory Brexiteers have been discussing his codicil to the Brexit withdrawal agreement: "It has become known as Cox's Codpiece." Oh dear. Yes, a Henry V reference here, of course, and a convenient way to introduce the absurdly pompous figure of Cox.'

Theresa May's EU deal was voted down overwhelmingly in the House of Commons, for the second time in as many months. The government lost by a margin of 149 votes. Although the prime minister had convinced about 40 Tory MPs to change their minds, it was not nearly enough to overturn the historic 230-vote defeat she had suffered in January.

13 March 2019
Steven Camley
Herald Scotland

16 March 2019
Morten Morland
The Times

Vince Cable said he would step down as the leader of the Liberal Democrats after the UK's local elections. 'I take pride in seeing the party recovering strongly, with last year's local election results the best in 15 years, record membership and a central role in the People's Vote campaign,' Cable said. Commentators pondered whether anybody would notice the change in leadership of the Commons' fourth-largest party, considering the crisis engulfing the government.

GUN CONTROL

In the wake of a far-right terrorist attack in New Zealand that left 51 people dead, Prime Minister Jacinda Ardern said her government would ban all types of semi-automatic weapons and assault rifles. Ardern said the attack – in which a white supremacist gunman opened fire on Muslims praying in Christchurch – had caused 'one of New Zealand's darkest days'.

23 March 2019
Ingram Pinn
Financial Times

The EU offered Theresa May a 16-day extension to her Brexit deal, with a new leaving date of 12 April. But commentators said that a short extension would not be enough to solve May's problems. Parliament had overwhelmingly voted down her deal twice, and in the face of continued opposition from the likes of Brexiteer MP Jacob Rees-Mogg, her premiership seemed increasingly untenable.

24 March 2019
Chris Riddell
Observer

As Theresa May's Brexit strategy went into meltdown, the People's Vote campaign said that nearly a million people had joined its latest anti-Leave march in London – making it among the biggest protests in British history. Protesters carrying EU flags and placards called for the government to put Brexit to another public vote.

24 March 2019
Brian Adcock
Independent

25 March 2019
Steve Bright
Sun

A group of senior ministers began plotting a coup to oust Theresa May as prime minister. The *Sunday Times* reported that at least 11 members of the cabinet backed the revolt, in which May would be replaced by either Michael Gove, Jeremy Hunt or David Lidington. The resurrection of Gove's fates came just two years after his prime ministerial ambitions were killed off during his disastrous 2016 leadership campaign.

Boris Johnson told Theresa May to 'channel the spirit of Moses' in order to deliver Brexit. He said that May should tell the EU, 'Let my people go'. In the Bible, the freeing of the Israelites was followed by 40 years' wandering in the wilderness – perhaps, in Christian Adams' view, an apt description of Brexit.

25 March 2019
Christian Adams
Evening Standard

MPs TAKE CONTROL...

27 March 2019
Peter Brookes
The Times

MPs took the unprecedented step of seizing control of the parliamentary timetable, in order to hold a series of 'indicative votes' on how to break the Brexit deadlock. While the move wrested control of Brexit from the beleaguered prime minister and her attorney general, Geoffrey Cox, it was unclear whether her critics – such as Boris Johnson, Jeremy Corbyn and John Bercow – would fare any better.

The speaker ruled that the government could not table the same proposition in the House of Commons twice. The decision was a blow to Theresa May, who had planned to hold a third 'meaningful vote' on her Brexit deal without amending it. But commentators said that even if May's deal were voted on a third time, it was still unlikely to pass.

28 March 2019
Steven Camley
Herald Scotland

The House of Commons voted down Theresa May's Brexit deal for a third time. With the prime minister's strategy in tatters, commentators reflected on where she had gone wrong. 'In clinging dogmatically to her Brexit red lines, Theresa May led negotiations around in the same circles,' says the cartoonist. 'Meanwhile, the entire country seemed to vanish into the monotone maelstrom of Brexit, entirely losing sight of what our many-hued continent was, or could be in future.'

28 March 2019
Ella Baron
Times Literary Supplement

Open warfare erupted in the cabinet over the way forward on Brexit. Rumours circulated that advocates of a soft Brexit – including the likes of Philip Hammond and David Lidington – were calling for an extension, while more hard-line MPs – including Dominic Raab, Michael Gove and Andrea Leadsom – had pivoted to supporting no-deal, with Theresa May stuck in the middle.

2 April 2019
Patrick Blower
Telegraph

4 April 2019
Peter Brookes
The Times

A video of paratroopers using a Jeremy Corbyn poster for target practice circulated on social media. The Ministry of Defence said the men in the video had been reprimanded, and that their behaviour was 'not fitting of the high standards we expect'. Meanwhile, Brexiteer MPs including Iain Duncan-Smith, Boris Johnson and Jacob Rees-Mogg continued to attack Theresa May – inadvertently drawing the Tories' fire away from Corbyn.

Theresa May made a last-ditch trip to Brussels to request an extension to Article 50, to prevent the UK crashing out of the EU without a deal. Commentators said that the key European figures – such as Angela Merkel, Emmanuel Macron, Donald Tusk and Jean-Claude Juncker – had little choice but to extend the deadline. 'What a relief to do a Brexit drawing where Theresa May barely appears,' says the cartoonist. 'Some of my colleagues, who draw several cartoons every week, must find it very difficult.'

9 April 2019
Peter Schrank
The Times

POLITICAL BLACK HOLE - FIRST PICTURES

©Steve Bell 2019-11·4- Belltoons.co.uk

11 April 2019
Steve Bell
Guardian

Benjamin Netanyahu looked set to hold on to power following elections in Israel. Although Netanyahu's right-wing Likud Party and the liberal Blue and White alliance tied with 35 seats each, smaller parties that had previously entered a coalition with Netanyahu seemed likely to deliver him a fifth term as prime minister. In other news, astronomers released the first-ever photo of a black hole.

The EU agreed to delay Brexit until 31 October: Halloween. European Council President Donald Tusk asked of his 'British friends . . . please do not waste this time.' With rumours circulating that Boris Johnson, Dominic Raab, Michael Gove and Sajid Javid were all planning leadership campaigns, May's days in Number 10 were numbered.

12 April 2019
Dave Brown
Independent

12 April 2019
Morten Morland
The Times

Wikileaks founder Julian Assange was arrested at the Ecuadorean embassy in London. Assange had been staying in the embassy since 2012, having sought asylum there to avoid being extradited to Sweden, where he faced rape allegations. Meanwhile, the increasingly embattled Theresa May continued to search for a solution to the Brexit crisis.

Nigel Farage launched his new Brexit Party, after it was announced that Britain would participate in the EU elections in May. 'I said that if I did come back into the political fray it would be no more Mr Nice Guy and I mean it,' said Farage. Left-leaning commentators asked when Farage had been 'Mr Nice Guy', noting his involvement in some of the most controversial campaigns in recent history – including leading UKIP to the right and alleging that Britain had been brought to 'breaking point' by migration.

13 April 2019
Ben Jennings
i

16 April 2019
Martin Rowson
Guardian

The government announced a tranche of reforms designed to bolster tenants' rights. The plans involved banning Section 21 notices, which allowed landlords to evict renters at short notice, without reason. The policy looked set to be one of Theresa May's final major policy announcements, with pro-Brexit MPs – including Boris Johnson and Jacob Rees-Mogg – becoming increasingly keen to boot her out of Downing Street.

A huge fire engulfed the medieval Cathedral of Notre-Dame in Paris. Dramatic footage showed fire ravaging the roof of the building, with the spire toppling into the flames. French President Emmanuel Macron vowed to rebuild the cathedral 'within five years'.

17 April 2019
Patrick Blower
Telegraph

17 April 2019
Christian Adams
Evening Standard

Labour vowed to scrap Sats exams in English primary schools. Jeremy Corbyn said that the tests, undertaken by seven- and 11-year-olds, contributed to a 'regime of extreme pressure testing'. The Labour leader's critics said that he should be focusing on his ambiguous policy on a second Brexit referendum, rather than on education.

The actor Emma Thompson was labelled a hypocrite after flying 5,400 miles to join an environmental protest in London. Thompson joined the group Extinction Rebellion in Oxford Circus, as they occupied sites across central London to call for government action on climate change.

20 April 2019
Peter Brookes
The Times

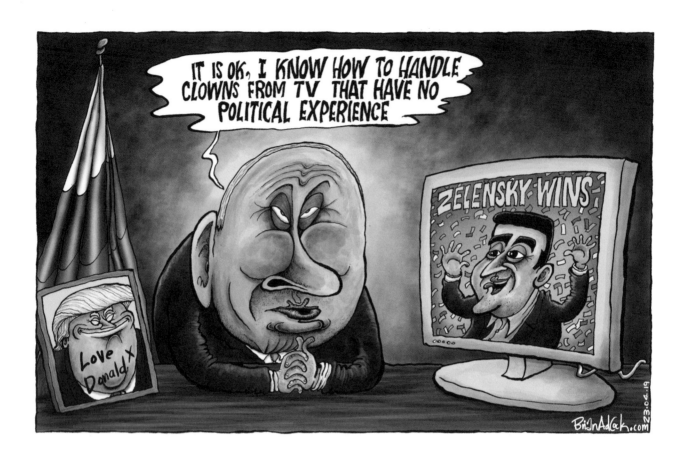

23 April 2019
Brian Adcock
Independent

Comedian Volodymyr Zelensky won a landslide victory in Ukraine's presidential election. Like Donald Trump, Zelensky made his name as a television star before becoming involved in politics – he acted in a TV show called *Servant of the People*, in which his character played the president. The incumbent president Petro Poroshenko said that Zelensky was too inexperienced to stand up to Vladimir Putin, who had designs on the region.

Former Conservative MP Ann Widdecombe announced she would return to front-line politics to join the Brexit Party. The former shadow home secretary said she backed Nigel Farage's party because she wanted the Tories to 'get on with it', saying Brexit had made Britain 'an international laughing stock' – a bit rich, some thought, considering Widdecombe's much-ridiculed appearance in the 2010 series of *Strictly Come Dancing*.

25 April 2019
Peter Brookes
The Times

26 April 2019
Andy Davey
Telegraph

The prime minister clung on to power following a meeting in which she was excoriated by backbench Tory MPs, who were lining up to support potential successors – such as Boris Johnson, Jeremy Hunt and Sajid Javid. 'Theresa May escaped censure – and a change of rules on votes of confidence – from the 1922 committee. But rumour had it that they wanted a clear statement of when she would be packing her bags for the sunlit uplands,' says the cartoonist. 'Meanwhile, Extinction Rebellion protesters glued themselves to the London Stock Exchange in protest at environmental inaction.'

NUCLEAR ROUNDABOUT

Kim Jong-un and Vladimir Putin met for the first time, just two months after the North Korean premier's ill-fated talks with Donald Trump. Kim was widely expected to call on the Russian president's help in ameliorating the effects of Western sanctions. While North Korea had always had frequent contact with Xi Jinping's China, commentators said that Kim's new diplomatic tour suggested his regime was growing in confidence – not least thanks to the progress of its nuclear weapons programme.

27 April 2019
Ingram Pinn
Financial Times

LEAKY GOVERNMENT...

28 April 2019
Morten Morland
The Times

Theresa May's beleaguered government was described by experts as 'one of the leakiest ever', after details of high-level discussions on national security were passed to the press. The conversations, reported by the *Telegraph*, related to concerns about Chinese telecoms firm Huawei supplying the UK's 5G data network. Commentators said that Theresa May lacked the authority to prevent leaks from within her own cabinet.

A London Marathon runner dressed as Big Ben got stuck at the finish line because his costume was too tall. A video showed Lukas Bates, who was attempting to break the world record for completing a marathon while dressed as a landmark, requiring help to fit the top of his costume underneath the finishing-line canopy – an appropriate metaphor, some thought, for parliament's last-minute inability to deliver Brexit.

29 April 2019
Christian Adams
Evening Standard

29 April 2019
Brian Adcock
Independent

Labour said they would force a parliamentary vote on whether to declare an 'environmental emergency', in the wake of mass protests about climate change. The decision came days after Theresa May declined to attend a meeting with teenage climate activist Greta Thunberg, leader of the international 'school strike' movement. The 16-year-old left an empty chair for May at the meeting, which was attended by other UK party leaders.

Gavin Williamson was sacked as defence secretary. The prime minister's spokesperson said she had 'lost confidence in his ability to serve', following allegations that he had leaked national security information about the Chinese telecoms company Huawei to the *Telegraph*. Williamson denied leaking the information.

2 May 2019
Morten Morland
The Times

7 May 2019
Nicola Jennings
Guardian

Both the Conservative and Labour parties remained deadlocked over the way forward on Brexit. Although Theresa May and Jeremy Corbyn continued to hold talks about a compromise that would lead to parliament voting for a Brexit deal, they were getting nowhere. And backbench MPs warned that any agreement the pair came to remained unlikely to pass through the House of Commons.

SUCCESS IN EUROPE...

Theresa May said she would take inspiration from Liverpool FC, in the wake of their extraordinary 4–0 win over Barcelona in the Champions League semi-final. The club won despite having been 3–0 behind on aggregate at the beginning of the match – leading the prime minister to quip that, even when it looks like 'your European opposition has got you beat', it is possible to come out on top.

11 May 2019
Ben Jennings
i

129

MAXIMUM PRESSURE

11 May 2019
Ingram Pinn
Financial Times

Donald Trump said he would impose new sanctions on Iran, as part of his campaign to exert 'maximum pressure' on the country. The development came a year after Trump withdrew from a deal to limit Iran's nuclear proliferation, and days after US Secretary of State Mike Pompeo visited Iraq to condemn alleged Iranian interference there. International governments urged the US to act with restraint towards the region.

A poll suggested that Nigel Farage's Brexit Party looked set to come first in the upcoming European elections. The poll, by Opinium for the *Observer*, placed the Brexit Party on 34 per cent, Labour second on 21 per cent, and the Tories fourth at 11 per cent – behind the Liberal Democrats. Analysts said that Theresa May's willingness to negotiate with Labour over Brexit was encouraging grassroots Tories to vote for Farage. Meanwhile, a teaser trailer for the clown-themed horror film *It: Chapter 2* was released.

12 May 2019
Chris Riddell
Observer

15 May 2019
Peter Brookes
The Times

A group of senior Conservatives wrote to Theresa May calling on her to stop negotiating with Jeremy Corbyn. In a letter, 14 Tory MPs warned May that she would 'split our party and with likely nothing positive to show for it' if she agreed a Brexit deal with Labour. May's supporters hit back that it was actually Brexiteer MPs – such as Andrea Leadsom, Boris Johnson and Jacob Rees-Mogg – who were dividing the party.

Theresa May planned to give MPs another opportunity to vote on her Brexit deal, despite it having been voted down three times already. Downing Street said that a vote was necessary in early June 'if the UK is to leave the EU before the summer parliamentary recess'. Brexiteer Tories responded to the news with horror, with one backbencher telling the *Sun*, 'She is trying to distract attention from the fact she has run out of road.'

16 May 2019
Dave Brown
Independent

DAVID SIMONDS 17.5.19.

17 May 2019
David Simonds
Evening Standard

With Theresa May coming under increasing pressure to resign, Boris Johnson announced he would run for the Tory Party leadership when she stood down. 'Of course I'm going to go for it,' he said in an interview. 'I don't think that is any particular secret to anybody.' Johnson – who infamously once got trapped on a zip-wire during a photo call at the 2012 Olympics – was only one of a number of Tory grandees expected to run.

TARZAN OF THE LIB DEMS

EUROPEAN ELECTIONS

21.5.19. DAVID SIMONDS

The former Deputy Prime Minister Michael Heseltine – nicknamed 'Tarzan' – had the Conservative whip suspended after saying he would vote for the Liberal Democrats in the upcoming European elections. A long-standing Europhile, Heseltine linked his decision with the government's Brexit policy: 'I cannot, with a clear conscience, vote for my party when it is myopically focused on forcing through the biggest act of economic self-harm ever undertaken by a democratic government,' he said.

21 May 2019
David Simonds
Evening Standard

Donald Trump banned American companies from sharing technology with the controversial Chinese company Huawei, in a move interpreted as part of his trade war with Xi Jinping's regime. The news came after tech companies including Google limited Huawei's access to their products, due to its alleged attempts to hack western corporations. The US president's move ramped up pressure on Theresa May to take action against Huawei, which was being considered for a lucrative 5G internet contract in the UK.

21 May 2019
Brian Adcock
Independent

The UK government brought in rules to limit the use of plastic straws. Under the new policy, supermarkets would be unable to sell straws, but they would remain available in pharmacies. It came following public pressure to limit access to single-use plastics. But the government's opponents said that the announcement was merely a distraction from Theresa May's more pressing problems – from the Irish backstop to calls for a second referendum on Brexit.

22 May 2019
Christian Adams
Evening Standard

22 May 2019
Ben Jennings
Guardian

A man was charged with assault for throwing a milkshake over Nigel Farage while he was out campaigning in Newcastle. The incident was only the latest in a series of milkshake-throwing controversies: the previous week, police had ordered a McDonald's near a Brexit Party rally to stop selling milkshakes, to limit the risk of such attacks. The same day, the EU announced they would investigate Farage for failing to declare thousands of pounds of expenses in his capacity as an MEP.

Theresa May resisted growing calls to resign, despite growing frustration with her beleaguered Brexit policy. May had angered Tory MPs by proposing yet another vote on her EU deal, which they said would not get through the House of Commons. But government sources said the prime minister had no intention of stepping down, and remained committed to delivering Brexit.

23 May 2019
Ian Knox
Belfast Telegraph

25 May 2019
Ben Jennings
i

Following intense pressure from within her own government and party, Theresa May announced her resignation as prime minister. In an emotional speech outside Downing Street, May outlined plans to stand down as Conservative leader in June, and said it was a matter of 'deep regret' that she had been unable to deliver Brexit. In the wake of her speech, a number of May's sternest critics – including Boris Johnson, Dominic Raab and Jacob Rees-Mogg – praised her for her 'duty' and 'dignity'.

The Conservative Party came fifth in the European parliament elections, in a disastrous night for the two main parties. The Tories were trounced by Nigel Farage's Brexit Party, which won 29 seats despite having only been founded six weeks previously. May described the results as 'very disappointing', saying they showed 'the importance of finding a Brexit deal'.

28 May 2019
Dave Brown
Independent

Despite a catastrophic showing in the European elections, in which Labour came third behind the Liberal Democrats, Jeremy Corbyn remained ambivalent about a second Brexit referendum and maintained that he would prefer a general election. 'The unseen Brexiteer hands of Corbyn's advisers – Seamus Milne, Len McCluskey etc. – were obviously at work here, making sure that there was no People's Vote and that we slipped out of the EU without consulting the people,' says the cartoonist. 'Planning for a general election, based on an electoral share of 14 per cent, reminded me of the old turkeys metaphor.'

30 May 2019
Andy Davey
Telegraph

Donald Trump praised Boris Johnson and Nigel Farage in advance of his state visit to the UK. 'Nigel Farage is a friend of mine, Boris is a friend of mine. They are two very good guys, two very interesting people,' the president said, before going on to praise Farage's Brexit Party. The comments came amid ongoing discussion of the likelihood of a UK–US trade deal after Brexit, which could see American goods – including chlorinated chicken products – being imported into the UK.

3 June 2019
Chris Riddell
Observer

4 June 2019
Patrick Blower
Telegraph

As Donald Trump arrived in the UK for a state visit, Jeremy Corbyn said he would not attend the state banquet held at Buckingham Palace in honour of the president. 'Theresa May should not be rolling out the red carpet for a state visit to honour a president who rips up vital international treaties, backs climate change denial and uses racist and misogynist rhetoric,' the Labour leader said. Corbyn's critics said he was hardly in a position to condemn the US president, considering his supposed links with the Venezuelan government and with militant groups like Hezbollah and Hamas.

Moments before landing in the UK, Donald Trump launched an attack on Sadiq Khan. After the Mayor of London released a video in which he said Trump's values 'are the complete opposite of London's', Trump tweeted that Khan 'is a stone cold loser who should focus on crime in London, not me'. Moments later, guns were fired from Green Park and the Tower of London in honour of Trump's arrival.

4 June 2019
Morten Morland
The Times

4 June 2019
Steven Camley
Herald Scotland

The Queen and Donald Trump praised the relationship between the UK and the US during a state banquet at Buckingham Palace. Queen Elizabeth said the 'special relationship' had ensured the 'safety and prosperity of both our peoples for decades'. Trump responded by calling the queen a 'great, great woman'.

Nigel Farage hailed the Brexit Party's 'big, big showing' at a by-election in Peterborough, despite his party coming second to Labour. Lisa Forbes narrowly retained the seat for Labour, in what Jeremy Corbyn hailed as an 'incredible' win for 'the politics of hope'. Commentators had said that Farage's new party was likely to win the seat, which had voted Leave by a large margin in the EU referendum.

7 June 2019
Christian Adams
Evening Standard

OUR POLICY IS HAVING OUR COKE AND NOT SNORTING IT

As the Tory leadership contest got underway, candidates were quizzed on whether they had taken drugs in the past. Michael Gove admitted to snorting cocaine decades previously, and journalists dug up footage of front-runner Boris Johnson on the BBC show *Have I Got News for You*, in which he said, 'I think I was once given cocaine, but I sneezed and so it did not go up my nose.' Among Johnson's many controversial statements was his 2016 quip about Brexit that 'Our policy is to have our cake and eat it.'

12 June 2019
Steve Bell
Guardian

Seven Tory leadership candidates – Dominic Raab, Boris Johnson, Rory Stewart, Jeremy Hunt, Matt Hancock, Michael Gove and Sajid Javid – secured enough MPs' votes to progress to the second round of the contest. Three candidates – Andrea Leadsom, Esther McVey and Mark Harper – were eliminated. Critics said that all of the candidates were 'chasing unicorns', instead of offering serious Brexit policies. 'Andrea Leadsom was originally dropping a placard saying "B******s", with reference to her own "Bollocks to Bercow" placard,' says the cartoonist. 'The *Guardian* made me remove this.'

14 June 2019
Nicola Jennings
Guardian

16 June 2019
Scott Clissold
Sunday Express

Theresa May refused to say which of the final five Tory leadership candidates – Michael Gove, Boris Johnson, Rory Stewart, Dominic Raab and Sajid Javid – she was backing. The prime minister told journalists, 'It's none of your business.' Commentators suggested that May was now so unpopular among the Tory membership that a public endorsement would actively hinder her chosen candidate.

Hundreds of thousands of people protested against a controversial extradition bill in Hong Kong. Opponents said that the bill, which would allow the authorities to deport people from Hong Kong to mainland China, would undermine the city's autonomy. Peter Schrank explains the rationale behind his cartoon, which riffs on a famous 1989 image of a man standing before a tank in Tiananmen Square. 'When quoting an image in a cartoon we should choose one that is familiar, then alter it in such a way that it remains recognisable – while at the same time adding a new twist,' he says. 'This one is not in the least bit funny. A cartoon doesn't necessarily have to be funny; it should merely provoke an emotional reaction.'

17 June 2019
Peter Schrank
The Times

18 June 2019
Brian Adcock
Independent

Tory leadership front-runner Boris Johnson refused to undertake any interviews or participate in live debates, while his rival candidates battled it out to make it into the final two. According to the cartoonist, 'Boris was keeping quiet as he is his own worst enemy, being the incompetent, lying, egotistical, narcissistic, inauthentic, unenlightened, privileged clown that he is. Hard keeping all that under wraps.'

SNP MP Ian Blackford branded Boris Johnson a 'racist' and said he was unfit to lead the country. During a debate in the House of Commons the SNP's Westminster leader highlighted previous comments Johnson had made about Muslims, Africans and Scots. While Blackford's attack would prove controversial, it was rather less dramatic than those suffered by some figures on the British right – many had recently been doused with milkshakes by left-wing activists.

20 June 2019
Steven Camley
Herald Scotland

21 June 2019
Peter Brookes
The Times

Boris Johnson and Jeremy Hunt were voted through to the final round of the Tory leadership campaign. Johnson, the former foreign secretary and a prominent Brexiteer, was the overwhelming favourite to win the contest, which was based on a vote of the 160,000 members of the Conservative Party.

ROUGHING UP RIVALS...

STOP BORIS

Boris Johnson's supporters had used tactical voting to keep Michael Gove off the final Tory leadership ballot, it was alleged. Newspapers reported that Johnson's team had advised MPs who wanted him to be leader to vote for Jeremy Hunt, to hand the former foreign secretary an easy win in the final round. In other news, the foreign office minister Mark Field was suspended from the government after slamming a female Greenpeace activist against a wall during a black-tie dinner in the City of London.

22 June 2019
Morten Morland
The Times

25 June 2019
Morten Morland
The Times

Jeremy Hunt, the underdog in the Conservative leadership race, called on his rival Boris Johnson not to be a 'coward' and to debate him on television. Sky News had pencilled in a debate between the two remaining candidates, but had cancelled it after Johnson dropped out.

Boris Johnson said that his hobby was to 'make models of buses'. Asked in an interview how he relaxed, the Tory leadership candidate said he likes to take 'wooden crates' and 'turn [them] into a bus . . . I paint the passengers enjoying themselves on the wonderful bus.' Responses ranged from amusement to cynicism, with some suggesting that Johnson's peculiar confession was a way of distracting from the recent high-profile dispute with his partner and his controversial Brexit strategy.

27 June 2019
Brian Adcock
Independent

29 June 2019
Ben Jennings
i

Donald Trump sparked controversy by joking with Vladimir Putin about their mutual dislike of journalists. 'Get rid of them,' the US president said to his Russian counterpart, while surrounded by press at a photo call at a G20 summit. Commentators reacted with anger at the quip, not least because scores of journalists had been murdered since the beginning of Putin's presidency. Meanwhile, as the Tory leadership campaign entered its final days, Boris Johnson was compared to Trump for allegedly calling the French 'turds' while foreign secretary.

FINE FEATHERED FRIENDS

Donald Trump become the first sitting US president to visit North Korea. Trump met with the supreme leader in the demilitarised zone between North and South Korea, before proceeding north into the insular state. Trump's critics said that the meeting was mere showboating, and that North Korea had yet to demonstrate a real commitment to denuclearisation.

1 July 2019
Seamus Jennings
Independent

1 July 2019
Steve Bright
Sun

Civil servants reportedly said that Jeremy Corbyn might have to stand down as leader of the opposition because of poor health. *The Times* quoted two senior Whitehall sources who thought Corbyn was 'too frail and is losing his memory'. Corbyn, 70, called the story a 'farrago of nonsense'. Meanwhile, with Boris Johnson's victory in the Tory leadership contest looking increasingly certain, commentators speculated on his fitness to be prime minister.

Boris Johnson and Jeremy Hunt both said that the Irish backstop had to be removed from any Brexit deal – despite the EU having repeatedly stated that this was not possible. Remainers suggested that the Tory leadership rivals' claims were utopian and unachievable. After this cartoon was published, Christian Adams came under fire for depicting the two men as leprechauns. According to Felix Larkin in the *Irish Times*, 'Adams' cartoon is but one in a series of recent cartoons which have offended public opinion because they are perceived to use negative stereotyping – in this instance, anti-Irish stereotyping.'

2 July 2019
Christian Adams
Evening Standard

3 July 2019
Dave Brown
Independent

Brexit Party MEPs turned their backs during the EU anthem at the official opening of the European Parliament. Nigel Farage said that his 29 MPs were 'cheerfully defiant' in resisting calls to face the front during the ceremony. A party spokesperson later told the press, 'We were delighted our message was heard across Europe today.'

Boris Johnson laid into the sugar tax – or 'sin tax' – that Theresa May had introduced. The levy, introduced in April 2018, aimed to tackle obesity by setting a minimum cost for sugary drinks. But Johnson said he was concerned that it unfairly targeted the poor. The original version of this cartoon was amended to obscure the word 'shitburger'.

4 July 2019
Dave Brown
Independent

Brexit Party MEP Ann Widdecombe compared Brexit to 'slaves' rising up 'against their owners'. During her maiden speech in the European Parliament, the former Tory MP said Britain's departure was part of a historical pattern of 'oppressed people turning against their oppressors' – a comparison that Remainers branded 'disgusting'. Steve Bell's cartoon riffs on the classic prohibitionist design 'Am I Not a Man and a Brother?'.

5 July 2019
Steve Bell
Guardian

HAIL TO THE CHIEF

Donald Trump held a military parade to mark Independence Day. As tanks processed through Washington D.C., the president addressed the nation from the Lincoln Memorial as part of a so-called 'Salute to America'. Trump's critics described the event as a vanity project, with the state legislature tweeting, 'We have said it before: Tanks, but no tanks.'

6 July 2019
Ingram Pinn
Financial Times

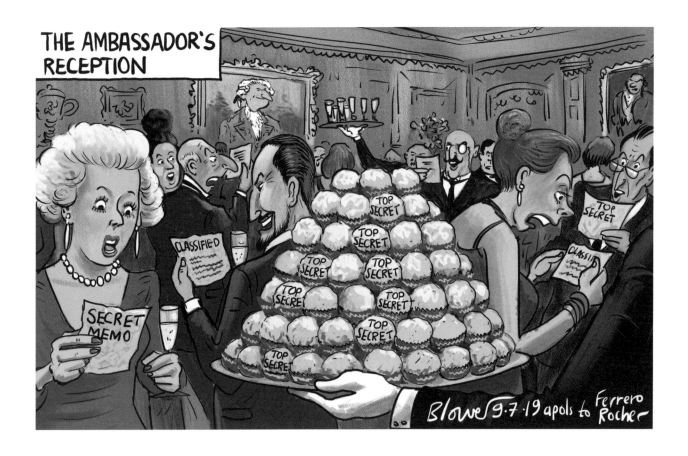

A tranche of leaked emails from the UK ambassador to the US sparked an international diplomatic row. In the emails, Kim Darroch described Donald Trump's administration as 'uniquely dysfunctional' as well as 'diplomatically clumsy and inept'. As the White House responded with outrage, saying it would sever ties with Darroch, journalists speculated about how the top-secret cable made it into the hands of the media.

9 July 2019
Patrick Blower
Telegraph

POLICY BREAKTHROUGH...

OUR POSITION IS NOW CLEAR...

WE RESERVE THE RIGHT TO CAMPAIGN FOR REMAIN...

AGAINST OUR OWN BREXIT DEAL...

UNITE

9.7.19 DAVID SIMONDS

Unions affiliated with the Labour Party reached an agreement with Jeremy Corbyn about their joint stance on Brexit. The new position, organised in part by Unite boss Len McCluskey, was that Labour would back a second referendum on any Tory Brexit deal. But critics said that the policy – in which the opposition reserved the right to campaign against a potential Labour-negotiated Brexit deal – was still too equivocal.

9 July 2019
Dave Simonds
Evening Standard

11 July 2019
Peter Brookes
The Times

Boris Johnson refused to back the beleaguered UK ambassador to Washington, Kim Darroch, during a televised Conservative leadership debate. Challenged six times on whether he would keep Darroch in his role, the former foreign secretary refused to rule out sacking him. Critics said that Johnson had thrown Darroch 'under a bus' – a fitting fate, perhaps, considering Johnson's famous hobby of making buses out of wooden crates.

Donald Trump tweeted, 'I don't have a racist bone in my body', after the House of Representatives voted to condemn him for attacking four congresswomen of colour. A resolution, passed by 240 votes to 187, criticised Trump's 'racist comments that have legitimised fear and hatred of New Americans and people of colour'.

18 July 2019
Steven Camley
Herald Scotland

20 July 2019
Peter Schrank
The Times

Donald Trump tweeted that four women of colour in the House of Representatives should 'go back' to the 'totally broken and crime infested places from which they came'. Trump's comments – made on the 50th anniversary of the first moon landing – were widely branded as racist: all four of the women are US citizens, and three were born in the USA. According to the cartoonist, 'I actually dislike drawing Trump. He is so awful as to be almost beyond the reach of satire. But there is also the fact that, although he is very thin-skinned, he thrives on courting controversy. So perhaps this is the way to do it. Draw him as a marginal figure, a small man on the edge of things, having things done to him.'

Chancellor Philip Hammond became the latest opponent of a hard Brexit to announce that he would not serve under Boris Johnson. As the Tory leadership campaign entered its final days, a number of former Remainers – including Amber Rudd, David Lidington and David Gauke – suggested they would not support a prime minister who backed no-deal. 'How many Conservatives would resign due to belligerent BoJo's bonkers Brexit plan?' asks the cartoonist. 'All of them, I hoped.'

22 July 2019
Brian Adcock
Independent

24 July 2019
Peter Brookes
The Times

Boris Johnson was elected leader of the Conservative Party, and consequently became prime minister. In his victory speech outside Number 10 Downing Street, Johnson promised to 'deliver Brexit, unite the country and defeat Jeremy Corbyn', saying, 'Like some slumbering giant we are going to rise and ping off the guy ropes of self-doubt and negativity.'

Boris Johnson expressed his opposition to the Irish backstop, describing it as 'divisive' and 'anti-democratic'. But the EU's chief Brexit negotiator, Michel Barnier, responded that the backstop was integral to any UK–EU deal, and that it was not possible to reopen negotiations. Commentators said that the backstop was likely to remain as much a problem for Johnson as it had been for May, who had ultimately been brought down by the issue.

26 July 2019
Christian Adams
Evening Standard

Look, Who's Chancellor..?

27 July 2019
Chris Duggan
The Times

Sajid Javid was appointed chancellor of the exchequer. The former home secretary – who had come fourth in the Tory leadership contest – is known for his admiration of Margaret Thatcher, even having had a portrait of her in his office.

Boris Johnson reiterated his opposition to the Irish backstop, while EU leaders including Angela Merkel and Jean-Claude Juncker continued to back it – ramping up the likelihood of a no-deal Brexit. According to the cartoonist, 'Boris Johnson is yet another example of how bad news can be great news for cartoonists. He is scary as hell, but presents a wonderfully broad front for us to attack. His self-serving recklessness, his lies, his blustering swagger. In this sense he is the exact opposite to Theresa May. She was desperately dull. We all clung to the image of her leopard-print shoes, the only thing that set her apart.'

28 July 2019
Peter Schrank
The Times

The pound plummeted to a two-year low against the dollar, after analysts concluded that a no-deal Brexit was increasingly likely. Boris Johnson's government had said it was willing to do 'whatever it takes' to leave the EU by 31 October, even if that involved walking away without an agreement. Commentators said that the turmoil on the currency markets would make life harder for British holidaymakers going abroad, as they would get noticeably less for their money.

31 July 2019
David Simmonds
The Times

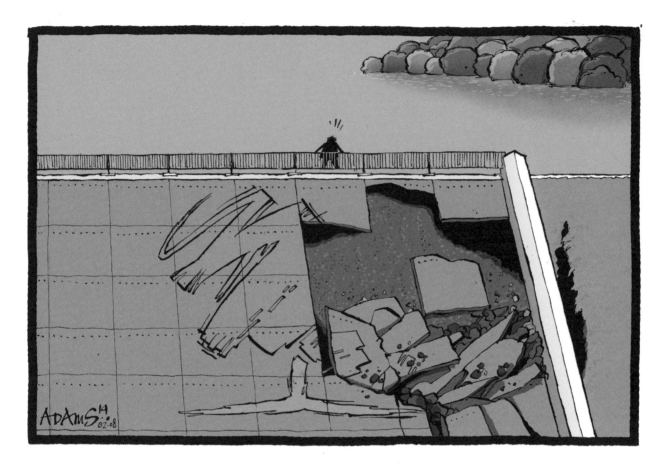

The Conservative Party lost the Brecon and Radnorshire by-election, leaving Boris Johnson with a working parliamentary majority of one. The Liberal Democrat candidate, Jane Dodds, overturned a Tory majority of over 8,000 to win the seat. Meanwhile, thousands of people were evacuated from a village in Derbyshire due to fears that the dam upstream of them was about to burst. A widely circulated image showed that part of the Whaley Bridge dam had collapsed, and commentators said that the whole structure was at risk of disintegrating.

2 August 2019
Christian Adams
Evening Standard

3 August 2019
Kevin Kallaugher
Economist

Boris Johnson told European leaders that Britain was prepared to leave the EU without a deal if it refused to renegotiate the withdrawal agreement. The prime minister released a statement saying, 'If we are not able to reach an agreement then we will of course have to leave the EU without a deal.' Andrew Adonis, the prominent pro-Remain peer, responded by saying that Johnson's policy was suicidal.

The newly appointed Home Secretary Priti Patel said she wanted criminals to 'feel terror' at the thought of breaking the law. Patel told the *Daily Mail*, 'I fundamentally think the Conservative Party is the party of law and order. Full stop.' The hard-line MP also denied ever having supported the death penalty, commenting, 'I have never said I'm an active supporter of it' – despite having told a 2011 *Question Time* audience that she 'would actually support the reintroduction of capital punishment' in some cases.

4 August 2019
Brian Adcock
Independent

The USA mourned in the wake of two mass shootings in 24 hours. Twenty-two people were killed when a 21-year-old white supremacist opened fire in a Walmart in El Paso, Texas; that evening, a man in Dayton, Ohio, murdered ten people in a bar. The twin attacks raised new questions about gun control in the US, with many arguing the constitutional right to bear arms should not endanger thousands of Americans each year.

5 August 2019
David Simonds
Sunday Times

John McDonnell said that the Labour Party would tell the Queen, 'We're taking over', if Boris Johnson lost a parliamentary no-confidence vote. Asked about what would happen if Boris Johnson refused to resign after losing the confidence of the House of Commons, McDonnell said he 'would be sending Jeremy Corbyn in a cab to Buckingham Palace'. Commentators had suggested that Corbyn could stand in as a caretaker prime minister until a no-deal Brexit was averted.

9 August 2019
David Simonds
The Times

SHRINKING...

STRONG 'N' STABLE

CRASH

Ben Jennings

10 August 2019
Ben Jennings
i

The UK economy shrank by 0.2 per cent in the second quarter of 2019, its first contraction since 2012. Economists said the surprise slowdown was due to a decrease in stockpiling, which many companies had begun in the build-up to the original Brexit date of 29 March. Labour blamed 'the Tories' Brexit bungling, including Boris Johnson now taking us towards no-deal' for Britain's economic woes.

Speculation mounted that Boris Johnson and his chief adviser Dominic Cummings were planning a general election, after the government announced a series of new policies – including 20,000 extra police officers and more money for the health service. According to the cartoonist, 'Boris tried to boost his electability with populist policies – completely inauthentic from the pompous Tory tosspot.'

12 August 2019
Brian Adcock
Independent

LOONEY TUNES...

14 August 2019
Morten Morland
The Times

One of Donald Trump's most senior advisers said that the UK was 'first in line' for a trade deal with the US. John Bolton, the president's moustachioed national security adviser, said that agreements could be struck 'very quickly' on a sector-by-sector basis. But commentators said that in return the UK may have to bow to a number of US trade demands, perhaps including putting the NHS on the table.

Philip Hammond launched a stinging attack on Boris Johnson, saying that a no-deal Brexit would be a 'betrayal' of the 2016 election result. In an article in *The Times*, the former chancellor said that the prime minister's call for the EU to abandon the Irish backstop was 'effectively a wrecking tactic'. He called on parliament to stop Britain crashing out without a deal.

14 August 2019
Christian Adams
Evening Standard

The Chinese government looked set to crack down on protestors in Hong Kong. Millions of people had taken to the streets to oppose a new extradition bill, which would have allowed suspects from Hong Kong to be extradited to the mainland. But after activists in an occupied airport building turned on police, there was speculation that the protestors – many of whom used umbrellas as a symbol of resistance – were about to be dispersed by the military.

14 August 2019
Patrick Blower
Daily Telegraph

There was a backlash against Liberal Democrat Leader Jo Swinson after she said that she would not back a caretaker government led by Jeremy Corbyn. The Labour leader had proposed toppling Boris Johnson and forming a 'government of national unity', which would prevent a no-deal Brexit in October and then call a general election. 'Jeremy Corbyn is a Brexiteer,' said Swinson. 'He cannot be trusted on Brexit.'

16 August 2019
Dave Brown
Independent

20 August 2019
Stephen Camley
Herald Scotland

Boris Johnson set off for Berlin and Paris, in an attempt to rally support from key EU figures for his approach to Brexit. The new prime minister intended to speak with the likes of Angela Merkel and Emmanuel Macron about how to stop Britain crashing out without a deal. Days previously, a leaked Whitehall dossier had suggested that the UK would face shortages of food, medicine and fuel in the event of a no-deal Brexit.

The leaders of the world's most powerful countries descended on the French seaside resort of Biarritz for a G7 summit. Donald Trump used the event to hail Boris Johnson as 'a person that's going to be a great prime minister'. But critics said that Johnson's burgeoning relationship with Trump might alienate key European leaders like Emmanuel Macron and Angela Merkel. 'This cartoon was published during the August bank holiday weekend. The forecast was for very warm and sunny weather,' says the cartoonist. 'So my brief to myself was to come up with a summery, cheerful image. I thought it would contrast nicely with the bleakness of the underlying message.'

25 August 2019
Peter Schrank
Sunday Times

On the pie label:
PORKY PIE
SEASONED AND INCURABLE
...BRITTLE CRUST
...HOT WATER AND
...COOKED UP
...BIG FAT
...H OF SALT

SINCE 2016

27 · 8 · 19

27 August 2019
Morten Morland
The Times

Boris Johnson inaccurately claimed that Britain sells Melton Mowbray pork pies to Thailand and Iceland. Speaking at the G7 summit, Johnson hailed the importance of a UK–US trade deal, saying the pies 'are sold in Thailand and in Iceland' but 'are currently unable to enter the US market because of . . . some sort of food and drug administration restriction.' The chair of the Melton Mowbray Pork Pie Association told the BBC that in fact no pork pies were exported to the two countries.

Boris Johnson prorogued parliament, thus undermining MPs' attempts to prevent a no-deal Brexit. 'Boris sent a deposition to Balmoral to request proroguing parliament in a bold manoeuvre to outplay the House of Commons,' says the cartoonist. 'It struck at parliamentary precedent and knocked over all sorts of protocols. Still, for the day at least, he seemed to have scored a hit. Outside, there was rage in the country. Polls suggested a large majority against proroguing and demonstrations happened spontaneously across many cities.'

29 August 2019
Andy Davey
Telegraph

31 August 2019
Peter Schrank
Sunday Business Post

Protestors took to the streets in the wake of Boris Johnson's decision to prorogue parliament. Hundreds of thousands of people took part in protests across 30 British towns, with participants saying they were motivated by the prime minister's disrespect for democracy. While Johnson maintained that his move had nothing to do with Brexit, commentators said that it was driven by his 'do or die' attitude to leaving the EU by 31 October.